the
Clean Eating
Meal Prep
cookbook

Easy Recipes & Time-Saving Plans for Healthy Living **On the Go**

Snezana Paucinac

Integrative Nutrition Health Coach

PAGE STREET
PUBLISHING CO.

PAGE STREET
PUBLISHING CO.

To all of you who have this book in
your hands:

May your life be filled with health
and happiness always.

May you find joy in cooking and taking
care of you and your loved ones.

Because you deserve it all.

With Love, SP

Contents

Introduction

My love for healthy food and cooking started about 12 years ago, after my second child was born. There came a point in my life where I decided it was time to start living healthier, so I started going to the gym and paying a little more attention to nutrition. The more I was aware of my body and the more I was tuned in, the better I felt. I truly discovered that there is something magical in listening to what your body needs and then supporting it through food.

Fast-forward five years. That love for nutrition led me to the Institute for Integrative Nutrition (IIN), where I got my nutrition and health coaching certification. I've spent the last seven years helping clients make small changes in their daily eating habits and, through that, achieve their health goals to ultimately become the best and healthiest versions of themselves.

Through my work with clients, I realized the one thing that was hardest for most of them was cooking meals during weekdays. Most of them went grocery shopping on Sunday and bought everything they liked and felt like eating at the moment. Once Monday came, the chaos started: not knowing what to eat for breakfast so grabbing just anything on the go, rushing home from work and trying to come up with a meal while hungry, and finally ending the day by bingeing on snacks late at night due to stress.

To help my clients get out of this vicious circle of eating, I highlighted the importance of meal preparation and good grocery shopping organization. Through my simple and delicious recipes, they discovered the joy of cooking and preparing meals for themselves and their loved ones. Food preparation and healthy eating became a way of life that gave them energy, strength and finally joy.

Making food should not induce stress; in fact, it should raise your energy and inspire joy. Preparing meals is such a natural habit for humans, yet we make it too complicated, so it becomes a burden. In today's busy world, we don't have time to cook every day or use recipes that contain 30 ingredients and take 75 minutes to make. Going back to real ingredients, simple foods and a variety of spices to tie it all together is where the happiness in cooking lies. And how does meal prep tie in to all of this? Read on.

By taking the time to plan and prepare meals ahead of time, you can avoid the stress and hassle of having to cook meals every day. Just imagine coming home from work to find that your dinner is either fully cooked or semi-prepared, and all you need is another 20 minutes to put it together and finish cooking it. And how about the fact that you won't need to raid your pantry while you wait for dinner to be ready? As you will see, your fridge can be fully prepared so that you will be nibbling on some great choices while you are wrapping up your meal-prepped dinner. Convinced yet? Let's continue.

When meal prepping, you are more likely to make healthier choices throughout the week, leading to a more balanced and nutritious diet. Meal prepping can also help you stick to a specific diet or fitness goal, as you can plan your meals to meet your nutritional needs. The best part is that you can control the ingredients and portion sizes—something that is hard to do when we eat in restaurants or grab something on the go. Also, by planning out your meals in advance, you will avoid last-minute trips to the grocery store or fast-food restaurants, saving you money and keeping you healthier.

I hope this cookbook inspires you to explore the world of clean, healthy eating, one recipe at a time. This meal prep cookbook will guide you to become efficient in meal preparation while keeping you healthy and happy, and that I can promise you.

With much love,

Snezana Paucinac

Meal Prep 101

Tips for Prepping and Storing Ready-to-Cook Ingredients

Let's start with the building blocks of successful meal prep: organized grocery shopping and keeping a well-stocked fridge and pantry.

Grocery shopping can be daunting and time-consuming. Sitting down and writing a grocery list will not only make the shopping trip less stressful but will also save you time. I like to sit down on Sunday mornings and think about the menu for the next week while I enjoy my coffee. For you that may be another time of day, but the idea is to prepare ahead and go with intention rather than wander around the store.

Now that we have organized our grocery list and gone grocery shopping, it is time to prepare some foods so that our cooking is much easier during the week. Because after all, the biggest part of cooking is the prep work. Some dishes can be lengthy because of the chopping we need to do; some are lengthy because of all the steps we need to take to cook the meal. I love making meatballs, but just thinking about having to form 12 or 24 of the mini ones makes me a bit stressed. I love a good stir-fried rice, but knowing that I need to chop all those veggies makes me rethink whether I really want to make that today. So this is where meal prep comes in!

In this chapter you will find guides on meal prep you can do ahead of time, such as prepping veggies, cooking grains in batches, making meat marinades, getting organized when grocery shopping and keeping the fridge well stocked and clean. These techniques will not only make your meal prep easier but will also influence you toward and support you in developing and keeping healthy habits.

Colorful, Nutrient-Dense Veggies

We should strive to eat a wide variety of fruits and vegetables every week due to the diversity of antioxidants that they contain. As a good rule of thumb, when you go grocery shopping, pick at least three different types of vegetables besides onions and garlic (those should be your base that you always have on hand). My usual grocery list includes peppers, cucumbers, tomatoes, white or purple cauliflower, zucchini, onions, carrots, garlic and sweet potatoes.

With the selection above, you are ready to cook pretty much anything! All of these veggies can be prepared ahead and stored in the fridge for easy use during the week. When the peppers are washed and cut, all you need to do is pull them out of the fridge to prepare a yummy Veggie Frittata with Feta (page 153) for breakfast. Your zucchini is spiralized already? Just add delicious Rustic Bolognese with Beef and Eggplant (page 45) for a yummy dinner option. And if you prepped the Bolognese already? Guess what? Your dinner is served!

Zucchini

Zucchini is very delicate and it goes bad easily, but proper preparation sure helps with that. Cutting the zucchini in thicker circles and then marinating it and storing it in a Ziploc® bag or glass container ensures the zucchini stays fresh and is ready to be grilled.

Some great marinade combinations for **grilled zucchini**:

- *Olive oil + thyme + Himalayan salt*
- *Olive oil + garlic powder + oregano + basil + Himalayan salt*
- *Olive oil + rosemary + Himalayan salt*
- *Olive oil + Dijon mustard + thyme*

Zucchini noodles, a.k.a. zoodles, take a bit of time when it comes to preparation, so it's really handy to make them ahead. To make the zoodles, you will need to use a spiralizer. You do not need to peel the zucchini to spiralize it—just cut both ends off. Once you make the zoodles, it is important to let them dry before storing them in a glass container. Place a paper towel in a colander, then add the zoodles in. Place another paper towel on top and let it rest for about 10 minutes. Once the zoodles are dry, take them out of the colander and place them in a glass container with a lid.

Another way to store zoodles is to bake them first. Once you make the zoodles and dry them as described above, place them on a baking sheet and spray some olive oil on top. Bake at 400°F (200°C) for about 20 minutes, or until the zoodles are tender. Allow the zoodles to cool down completely, and then transfer them to a storage container with a lid. Store them in the fridge for about 3 days.

Suggested Recipes: Grilled zucchini is a really easy add-on to any protein you have left over, like for example Grilled Chicken Fajitas with Peppers and Onions (page 113), Juicy Baked Chicken Parm (page 42), Baked Turkey Meatballs with Mint Yogurt Sauce (page 65) or even Miso-Glazed Tofu Wrap (page 97). Grilled zucchini is also a great option to add to some of the wonderful meal prep bowls in the California Bowls section (page 127).

Peppers

Did you know **peppers** contain more vitamin C than lemons? Yep! Colorful peppers are a great choice not only for a veggie to add to your lunch or dinner but also for breakfast and snacks.

As part of your weekly meal prep, cut peppers in strips and place them in a storage container or Ziploc® bag. Store them in the fridge for up to 4 days. Prepared peppers like this will come in handy for some delicious recipes such as Grilled Chicken Fajitas with Peppers and Onions (page 113), Spring Rolls with Tofu and Peanut Butter Sesame Dressing (page 83) and Veggie Frittata with Feta (page 153) and Shrimp Fried Rice (page 101).

Roasted red peppers are such a great add-on to salads. Once you start reading Italian and Greek recipes, you will see that they show up often. In Serbia, roasted red peppers are a staple salad you can find in many restaurants. Below I am sharing one simple way you can prepare roasted red peppers and keep them in the fridge for a full week. And be sure to try the White Bean and Roasted Red Pepper Salad (page 34)—it may become one of your favorites!

To roast the peppers, simply wash them and pat them dry with a paper towel. Line a baking sheet with foil, then add the peppers. You can add as many peppers as you can fit on your pan. Turn on the broiler at the highest setting and broil them on one side until the tops of the peppers look roasted (the skin will start lifting up). Flip them to the other side and broil them for the same amount of time. Depending on the heat of your oven, this process may take 20 to 30 minutes. Once the peppers are roasted on both sides, wrap foil around them tightly and let them rest for about 10 minutes. Peel off the skin and take out the stems. You may wash off any seeds that are left on the peppers. Once the peppers cool down completely, place them in a storage container in the fridge. If you wish, you can freeze the peppers at this point. Use them within 3 months, and to defrost them, just leave them at room temperature overnight.

To make a traditional Serbian roasted red pepper salad, clean the peppers and place them in a single layer in a large rectangular storage container. Add some olive oil, apple cider vinegar and Himalayan salt. Add some crushed garlic and fresh parsley. Add another layer of peppers, and repeat all the steps until you have used all the peppers. Cover them with the lid and store them in the fridge for a full week.

Carrots, Onions, Leeks and Celery

These four veggies are your main ingredients for almost any soup or stew. I am sure there have been many times when you wanted to make a hearty stew but then remembered that you needed to chop the onions, dice the carrots, slice the leeks and chop the celery. That is a lot of chopping, I know! Now of course you can buy all these and many other veggies prewashed and precut, but in the long run that is not the most economical option. When you're in a rush, though, it's a great alternative.

If you wish to keep them fresh and crisp for more than 3 days, celery, carrots and leeks are best chopped, cubed or sliced and stored in a glass container with water. If you are storing them just for the next day, you may keep them in a Ziploc® bag or reusable silicone bag. For a wonderful fresh veggie snack, cut the celery into small, finger-sized ribs and quarter the carrots. Place them in a jar and fill it up with the water to the top. Store it in the fridge for up to 5 days.

Onions should be stored separately from other vegetables, especially when cut, as they contain ethylene gas, which can cause produce to ripen faster. Once you dice the onions, place them in a storage container with a lid and store them in the fridge for up to 5 days.

Butternut Squash, Spaghetti Squash and Pumpkin

While storage for this trio is not a problem, as they store well at room temperature, preparation is where things get tricky. All of these vegetables take a long time to clean and prepare, so a little advance work goes a long way.

Peel the **butternut squash or pumpkin**, cut it into cubes and store it in a Ziploc® bag or a storage container with a lid and place it in the fridge for up to 3 days. If you wish, you can also bake the butternut squash by spraying it with some olive oil and baking it at 425°F (220°C) for about 30 minutes or until it's easy to poke with a fork. Once it cools down completely, transfer it to a storage container and place it in the fridge.

Baked butternut squash like this can be used as an easy veggie side dish or as a salad topping. The Fall Harvest Bowl with Roasted Butternut Squash, Apples and Walnuts (page 143) becomes a super-fast lunch bowl if you prep the butternut squash ahead of time!

Spaghetti squash is such a great alternative to flour- or grain-based spaghetti. To prepare it, cut the spaghetti squash in half and place it cut side down on a sheet pan. Bake it at 425°F (220°C) for about 45 to 50 minutes. While it's hot, take a spoon and scoop out the seeds. Then take a fork and scrape the squash to make the spaghetti. Place it in a glass container and allow it to cool down completely, then cover it and store it in the fridge over the next 5 days.

Prepared spaghetti squash is great with Juicy Baked Chicken Parm (page 42), Rustic Bolognese with Beef and Eggplant (page 45), Hearty Homestyle Meatballs (page 50) and Blueberry Kale Smoothie (page 171).

Fresh Greens, Microgreens and Herbs

Nutrient-dense and antioxidant-packed leafy greens are always good to have on hand. No matter what you choose to prepare, there is always some space to add in greens. I like buying the packaged kinds such as arugula, spinach, romaine and kale during the week and adding in fresh greens from the farmers' market on the weekend.

Fresh greens such as spinach, kale, collard greens, butter lettuce or any other type of lettuce are best kept unwashed in the fridge, as they will last longer. Alternatively, you may wash the greens, dry them well, wrap them in a paper towel and store them in a container with a lid. As the top and the back of the fridge are always the coldest, avoid stocking those areas with any leafy greens, as there is a chance of frost. I am sure it has happened to you quite a few times: you pull out a bag of spinach and it looks like it has defrosted!

Fresh herbs add so much flavor to just about any dish we make, so having some on hand at all times is a great idea. Herbs that have soft green stems, such as parsley, basil and cilantro, are best stored in the fridge in a small jar with some water at the bottom. You do not need to wash the herbs before placing them stem-first in the water—just trim the bottoms of the stems a little bit. The herbs with harder brown stems—such as thyme, rosemary and oregano—can last a little longer in the fridge as they are hardier. These herbs you can wash, pat dry and wrap in a paper towel, then store in a storage container with a lid.

I also love buying herbs in small pots. These can be stored on the kitchen counter for a long time as long as you water them according to the instructions. Basil and oregano are the two I buy like this most often.

Freezing fresh herbs is also a great option. For this you will need a silicone ice cube tray, as they work the best. Wash the herbs well and pat them dry with a paper towel. Chop the herbs and place them at the bottom of the tray. Fill the tray with water, just enough to cover the herbs. Freeze them for a few hours, at least 3. Take the ice cubes out, place them in a Ziploc® bag and store them in the freezer over the next 3 to 6 months. To defrost them, add the ice cubes to a bowl and let them thaw. The herbs will be as fresh as they'd be if you just bought them! If you use fresh herbs in your soups and stews, you can also add olive oil instead of water. Freeze them the same way as you would if you used water, then add them straight to the pan or pot when it's time to defrost them.

Microgreens are young vegetable or herb greens that are harvested in their tiny sprout form. Although they're tiny, they are nutrient dense, are pretty when plated and add so much flavor to a dish. Some of my favorite microgreens include sunflower, basil, amaranth, daikon radish, alfalfa and arugula.

Microgreens are best kept in the containers or bags they come in when you buy them. Just like leafy greens, they should be kept away from the top shelf and the back of the fridge to avoid frost.

Grains and Legumes

Grains and legumes are not only nutritious, but they also add so much more depth to meals. They are rich in both protein and fiber, so using them in meals is very beneficial when it comes to keeping us full and managing our health.

Cereal, Gluten-Free Grains and Pseudograins

Oats are a special type of cereal grain that come from the edible seed of oat grass. The most commonly found are rolled oats or steel-cut oats. Rolled oats cook faster, so anytime you need breakfast ready fast, opt for this kind. Steel-cut oats require longer cooking as they are a much hardier grain, but they are so worth it if you ask me. Oats are also much more economical if you buy them in bulk. As a simple cooking rule, use a 1:2 oats-to-liquid ratio.

Similar to oats, **wheat** is also a type of cereal grain. Over the last decade, wheat has been getting a bad rap, mainly because it contains gluten. Not all wheat is the same: Certain types of wheat can very well be beneficial for those who can digest gluten. When picking wheat products, opt for whole wheat or whole grain varieties. Whole grain varieties include barley, corn and rye. Whole grain varieties are very good for our digestive systems as they are rich in protein as well as fiber. Whole wheat and whole grain products such as pastas and breads are superior to white flour kinds as they are made from the whole grain, which is not only more nutritious but also less processed.

If you are sensitive to gluten, there are plenty of **gluten-free grains and pseudograins** to choose from: amaranth, buckwheat, quinoa, corn, flax and millet are few examples. Some specialty flours such as chickpea flour, bean flour, potato flour, oat flour, rice flour, arrowroot, tapioca, teff and soy are also wonderful choices that do not contain gluten.

Quinoa and Rice

As a general rule, when grocery shopping, opt for at least one type of white rice, either basmati or jasmine, and one brown kind, as well as quinoa. Of course, if you prefer one type of rice then stick with that, or if quinoa is your preferred type of grain, just add that to your list. Both rice and quinoa are much cheaper when you buy them in bulk or in large bags, and since they are very stable pantry items, buying bigger quantities will not be a problem. As opening and closing bigger bulk packaging may affect the freshness of the grains, I suggest using smaller jars or Tupperware® containers to store these grains once you bring them home. Simply transfer some of the rice or quinoa to a storage jar, which you will keep handy, and then tightly close the bulk bag and place it at the back of the pantry for later use.

Quinoa and rice are wonderful to prepare ahead because they store really well in the fridge and in the freezer. Rice can even be stored at room temperature for up to 3 full days! To heat it up to use plain as a side dish, just microwave it for a minute or so or warm it up in a steam oven. It comes out as fluffy as if you just made it fresh!

Storage and Reheating: Cool down the grains completely and freeze them in 1-cup (240-g) portions (flattened in one layer) in silicone or Ziploc® bags. When ready to use the quinoa or rice, take the bag out of the freezer and defrost it at room temperature. To heat it up, either add it directly to the desired dish or use a glass bowl and warm it up in the microwave or steam oven.

On the following pages, you'll find two recipes for how to prepare perfectly fluffy quinoa and rice. If you use the recipes as described, your quinoa and rice will come out great every time.

Basic Quinoa

Yield: 4 cups cooked

1¼ cups (213 g) quinoa
2½ cups (600 ml) water

Add the quinoa and water to a small pot and bring it to a boil. Cover and cook the quinoa for about 16 minutes, or until all the liquid evaporates. Remove it from the heat, open the lid, add a paper towel on top of the pan and place the lid back on. Let it rest for about 10 minutes. This paper towel trick will remove all the excess moisture.

Suggested Recipes

Quinoa is great to add to almost any of the California Bowls (see page 127) as extra plant-based protein. Add it as a side dish to Grilled Chicken Fajitas with Peppers and Onions (page 113), Juicy Baked Chicken Parm (page 42), Pan-Seared Whitefish Filets in Tomato Sauce (page 40), Baked Turkey Meatballs with Mint Yogurt Sauce (page 65) or Turkey Chili (page 107).

Basic White Rice

Yield: 4 cups cooked

2 cups (400 g) rice
3 cups (720 ml) water

Add the water to a small pot and bring it to a boil. Wash the rice thoroughly, then add it to the water. Once it boils, cover it with the lid, lower the heat and cook it for about 20 minutes. When you remove it from the heat, fluff the rice with a fork, then leave it to rest for about 10 minutes.

Basic Brown Rice

Yield: 4 cups cooked

2 cups (400 g) rice
4 cups (960 ml) water

Add the water to a small pot and bring it to a boil. Wash the rice thoroughly, then add it to the water. Once it boils, cover it with the lid, lower the heat and cook it for about 25 minutes. When you remove it from the heat, fluff the rice with a fork and then leave it to rest for about 10 minutes.

Some Cooking Tips

When making any type of fried rice, it's best to use rice that's at least one day old to prevent the dish from coming out soggy. In case you happen to have freshly made rice, just let it cool down to room temperature by spreading it out on a baking sheet. To cool it down faster, you may place it in the freezer for a few minutes as well. This is a tip my best friend gave me a few years ago, and it truly changed my whole rice game!

Suggested Recipes

Basmati and jasmine rice are wonderful additions to Tofu Cabbage Curry (page 84), Baked Teriyaki-Glazed Chicken Wings (page 87) or Baked Chipotle-Lime Salmon (page 124). Choose whole grain or round grain rice for Bibimbap with Juicy Sirloin, Cucumbers, Shiitake Mushrooms and Carrots (page 88) or for Shrimp Fried Rice (page 101). Brown rice goes well in all the dishes above and is also a great add-on to any of the California Bowls (page 127).

Lentils, Beans and Chickpeas

Legumes such as lentils, beans and chickpeas are also shelf-stable, so buying larger quantities is cost-efficient. They're true gems when it comes to meal prep, especially because they can be bought in cans or jars already cooked. Just drain and rinse them, and they are ready to be used in recipes!

Lentils can also be bought cooked, but since they cook in less than 30 minutes, it's easy enough to prepare them ahead and store them in the fridge for later use.

Beans and chickpeas take a much longer time to cook, so buying them precooked is a much better option. If you prefer to cook them, soak them in water overnight, then boil them the next day. Beans may take from 45 minutes to up to 90 minutes to cook depending on the variety, and chickpeas take about 45 to 60 minutes to cook. Once they are cooked, drain them, allow them to cool down completely and place them in glass containers in the fridge.

Basic Lentils

Yield: 2–2½ cups cooked

1 cup (192 g) green lentils
2½ cups (600 ml) water

Suggested Recipes

Rice and Lentils with Caramelized Onions (page 119), Stuffed Zucchini Boats with Rice and Chickpeas (page 59), Curried String Beans with Chickpeas (page 94), Turkey Chili (page 107), and Baked Shrimp and Beans (page 111).

Add the water to a small pot and bring it to a boil. Wash the lentils thoroughly and then add them to the water. Once it boils, cover the pot with the lid, lower the heat and cook the lentils for about 25 minutes. Check to see if the lentils are tender, then strain them through a colander.

Allow the lentils to cool down completely, then transfer them to a storage container or a silicone bag. To freeze them, flatten the lentils in the silicone bag and freeze it. Defrost the lentils at room temperature or run them under hot water.

Protein

Protein is one of the essential macronutrients that are really important as part of a healthy diet. Whether you choose a plant-based protein source such as tofu or lentils or an animal-based one such as chicken or fish, opt to always have at least two to three different varieties on hand, either prepared ahead or ready to eat.

Ready-to-eat protein sources can be found in jars, cans or cartons and are really convenient when we need to prepare a meal on the fly. Some of my favorites include lentils, chickpeas, beans and artichokes, but peas, mushrooms and greens beans can also be found in cans as well as glass jars. Of course, you do not need to have all of these on hand at all times. I typically store chickpeas and beans, as I use them the most.

One important thing to remember when buying jarred or canned foods is to look at the ingredients label and ensure that there is nothing besides the main ingredients, water and perhaps salt. At times companies add sugar and different additives to canned or jarred goods for a more stable shelf life, but we should stay clear of those. If buying cans, look for a BPA-free label on the front or back of the can, as this chemical is often used in can and plastic manu-facturing, and it is not optimal for our health.

Marinating meat not only gives meat so much flavor, but it also prevents the meat from drying out when cooking. Mix the marinade ingredients together and pour it over the meat. Place it in a silicone or Ziploc® bag and then into the fridge for at least 30 minutes or overnight.

There are four ways to marinate chicken in order to preserve its juiciness:

Using lemon in the marinade. Lemon, because of the acidic properties of citrus, not only softens the meat but actually starts the cooking process as well. I like to combine lemon and olive oil and add any spices that I like to it, most often salt, oregano or basil and garlic powder. That is my basic trio when it comes to seasoning meat (check out my Zesty Lemon Marinade [page 17])!

Using mustard. Just like with lemon, rubbing mustard on the chicken tenderizes the meat so its juiciness is preserved and the cooking time is shortened (check out my Dijon Mustard Marinade [page 17]).

Using yogurt. Yogurt is another wonderful tenderizer that is often used in Greek and Middle Eastern cooking techniques. Simply add the yogurt and spices that you like and let the chicken rest overnight or at least for a few hours. The next day, grill the chicken as you usually would (check out my Creamy Dill-Citrus Marinade [page 17]).

Using olive oil and spices. This is not only a good trick to tenderize the chicken but also helps keep the chicken fresh in the fridge longer. The olive oil and spices are acting like a preservative in this case. The spices you use are up to you, but the gyro spice in Grilled Chicken Gyros with Homemade Gyro Spice (page 72) is wonderful and a true must-try!

All three of the following marinades can be used with chicken and turkey. For beef, pork and veal, use the olive oil and mustard-based marinades, as yogurt doesn't agree with red meats.

Zesty Lemon Marinade

¼ cup (60 ml) olive oil + 1 lemon + fresh herbs (thyme, oregano, basil, rosemary)

Dijon Mustard Marinade

¼ cup (60 ml) Dijon mustard + 2 tbsp (30 ml) olive oil

Creamy Dill-Citrus Marinade

½ cup (120 ml) yogurt + ½ lemon + fresh herbs (such as dill)

Fish cooks faster than other proteins, so marinating it is not necessary. **Shellfish** such as shrimp also cooks fast, but marinating it allows for even deeper flavor. Be sure to try Grilled Shrimp Tacos with Homemade Salsa (page 120), and you can use the same spices to make fish tacos as well!

Plant-based protein such as **tofu** does need a little bit of work so that it tastes just right. Tofu is very neutral in taste, so you can doctor it up to your liking easily. One of my favorite ways to prepare tofu is with a miso marinade, which you will find in the Miso-Glazed Tofu Wrap recipe (page 97). Here are three more easy marinades that you will love:

Sesame Ginger Marinade

1 tbsp (15 ml) sesame oil + ½ tsp ginger powder + ½ tsp garlic powder

Turmeric Chili Marinade

1 tbsp (15 ml) olive oil + ½ tsp turmeric powder + ½ tsp gochugaru chili flakes

Mexican Taco Marinade

1 tbsp (15 ml) olive oil + ½ tsp cumin + ½ tsp chili powder blend + ½ tsp garlic powder

When buying tofu, organic and non-GMO is the way to go; 80 percent of the soy-based products that are imported or grown in the USA are genetically modified. When searing tofu, pick the *firm* kinds, and for soups and stews you can buy *silken*, which is a bit softer.

Good Fats

Not only do good fats keep us full, but they are also excellent for our skin as well as for our mental health. From olives and avocados to nuts and seeds such as chia and flax to salmon and sardines, there are many sources of healthy fats, so surely there is something for everyone to choose from.

When choosing **olive or avocado oil**, ensure that you buy pure olive oil as sometimes olive oil can be mixed with other oils, compromising its quality and health benefits. One cost-efficient way to buy olive oil for cooking is to buy it in large containers and then use a small reusable glass bottle at home. For salads or anything where olive oil is used at the end of cooking, use finer kinds that usually come in smaller bottles. Olive oil is best when stored at room temperature.

Buy **nuts and seeds** in bulk for normal use, but buy in smaller quantities when optimal freshness is desired. It is best to store them in glass jars in the fridge. If you decide to buy larger quantities, you can freeze them in smaller Ziploc® bags and extend their freshness and expiration date for about 4 months, as they will stay fresh in the fridge for about 1 to 2 months. **Nut butters** are best when kept in the pantry, and oil separation is normal—just stir the nut butter to mix it.

Flax, chia and hemp seeds, if whole, can be stored in the pantry, but ground kinds are best kept in the fridge once you open them.

Everyday Fridge Staples

Keeping the fridge clean, organized and well stocked is very important when it comes to efficient meal prepping.

Every week, pick one day where you go through the fridge, clean it and reorganize it to get it ready for the new week. If you plan meals and grocery shop according to that schedule, at the end of the week you will have minimal cleanup.

Keeping the fridge well stocked doesn't mean having many things but rather having the right things. Depending on your dietary preferences, these items will vary, but as a general rule, you should always make sure to stock up on any grocery items that you use in cooking on a weekly basis. Think about the plant-based milk or coconut water you add to your smoothies (page 171), the eggs you love for breakfast, your favorite salad mixes and healthy snacks.

As you will see in the recipes in this cookbook, a variety of mustards and vinegars and soy sauce are just a few of the ingredients that repeat often. These grocery items have a very long shelf life, so you don't have to worry about them getting spoiled, but of course check the labels from time to time. We've all found that expired jar of pesto tucked in the back of the fridge!

Weekly Meal Plans

A great way to start meal planning is by following a well-organized meal plan. Evidence suggests it takes 21 days to form a new habit, so I put together four nutritionally dense weekly meal plans in order to set you up for success!

You do not need follow the weeks in order, and feel free even to swap the days around. At the end of the day, these are just four versions of a weekly meal plan, and you can play around and make the daily choices work for you. The meal plans will tell you which meals are planned for each weekday, but you can find more detailed instructions on meal prep and storage in the recipes themselves.

If you are a vegetarian or vegan, simply swap out meals with meat or fish and pick your favorite plant-based dish to add instead.

These four weekly meal plans will also come in handy any time you need to reset or simply feel like having a fresh start. My favorite times of the year to reset are after all the holidays in wintertime or after a busy summer.

These meal plans do not include snacks, but there are some great options in this cookbook when it comes to healthy snack options. Also, these are great choices to add to your meal planning if you need some extra calories due to strenuous workouts. Here are some of my favorites:

• *Miso-Glazed Tofu Wrap (page 97)*

• *Tuna Salad Seaweed Wrap (page 98)*

• *Spring Rolls with Tofu and Peanut Butter Sesame Dressing (page 83)*

• *Two-Ingredient Dough Flatbread Pizza (page 53)*

Also, the California Bowls section of this cookbook (page 127) contains some delicious, mostly plant-based meal choices that are great for bring-to-work lunches, quick post-workout meals or afternoon snacks if you know dinner won't be until later.

As you read through the meal plans below, you will see that some of the meals will be fully prepared ahead of time. Some will even get tastier as the flavors marinate over the few days that they are stored in the fridge. Great examples of this are Rustic Bolognese with Beef and Eggplant (page 45), Turkey Chili (page 107), Dairy-Free Spanakopita with Tofu and Spinach (page 76), and any of the stews or soups. Beyond the meal plans below, here are some other dishes that you will find to be true lifesavers during the week if you prepare them on weekends: namely the Hearty Homestyle Meatballs (page 50), Vegetarian Lasagna with Tofu, Spinach and Ricotta (page 35), and Curried String Beans with Chickpeas (page 94).

You'll also have some days where you plan to cook dinner that night. On those days, you will split the meal into two portions, so that you can enjoy the second portion the day after. This is where "cook it once, eat it twice" comes into play!

Depending on your schedule, you may go grocery shopping on the weekend for the whole week, or you may split the grocery shopping into two days and complete half on the weekend and the other half midweek. If your work week starts on a Monday, set aside a couple hours on Sunday to grocery shop and cook your meals for Monday. In my own experience, Mondays somehow surprise us every week, so getting organized on the weekends and taking away some of the Monday blues and stress truly helps!

Week 1

Meal Plan

Maple Quinoa Porridge with Cashew Milk (page 163)

High Protein Fagioli Soup with Chickpea Pasta (page 39)

Shrimp Fried Rice (page 101)

Moussaka with Ground Turkey, Zucchini and Potatoes (page 66)

Corn Muffins with Prosciutto and Feta (page 156)

Grilled Chicken Fajitas with Peppers and Onions (page 113)

Turkey Chili (page 107)

Overnight Oats Three Ways (page 168)

Weeknight Taco Skillet with Grass-Fed Beef (page 123)

Monday

Breakfast: Prep Maple Quinoa Porridge with Cashew Milk (page 163), eat 1 serving fresh and store the rest in individual single-portion containers in the refrigerator.

Lunch: Prep High Protein Fagioli Soup with Chickpea Pasta (page 39), eat 1 serving fresh and store the rest in a glass container in the refrigerator.

Dinner: Prep Shrimp Fried Rice (page 101), eat 1 serving fresh and store the rest in a glass container in the fridge for the next day.

Tuesday

Breakfast: Eat 1 serving of prepped Maple Quinoa Porridge with Cashew Milk (page 163).

Lunch: Eat 1 serving of prepped Shrimp Fried Rice (page 101).

Dinner: Prep Moussaka with Ground Turkey, Zucchini and Potatoes (page 66), eat 1 serving fresh and store the rest in a glass container in the refrigerator.

Wednesday

Breakfast: Prep Corn Muffins with Prosciutto and Feta (page 156), eat 1 serving fresh and store the rest in a glass container in the fridge.

Lunch: Eat 1 serving of prepped High Protein Fagioli Soup with Chickpea Pasta (page 39).

Dinner: Prep Grilled Chicken Fajitas with Peppers and Onions (page 113), eat 1 serving fresh and store the rest in a glass container in the fridge for the next day.

Thursday

Breakfast: Eat 1 serving of prepped Corn Muffins with Prosciutto and Feta (page 156).

Lunch: Eat 1 serving of prepped Grilled Chicken Fajitas with Peppers and Onions (page 113).

Dinner: Prep Turkey Chili (page 107), eat 1 serving fresh and store the rest in a glass container in the fridge for the next day.

Friday

Breakfast: Prep Overnight Oats Three Ways (page 168) and store the rest in individual single-portion containers in the refrigerator.

Lunch: Eat 1 serving of prepped Turkey Chili (page 107).

Dinner: Have a Friday fiesta! Prep Weeknight Taco Skillet with Grass-Fed Beef (page 123), eat 1 serving fresh and store the rest in individual single-portion containers in the refrigerator.

Week 2

Meal Plan

Overnight Oats Three Ways (page 168)

Italian Wedding Soup with Turkey and Quinoa (page 33)

One-Pan Mexican Rice with Chicken (page 108)

Baked Chipotle-Lime Salmon (page 124)

Baked Polenta with Spinach and Tofu (page 160)

Stuffed Zucchini Boats with Rice and Chickpeas (page 59)

Baked Turkey Meatballs with Mint Yogurt Sauce (page 65)

Boiled Egg Breakfast Bowl (page 159)

Baked Shrimp and Beans (page 111)

Monday

Breakfast: Prep Overnight Oats Three Ways (page 168), eat 1 serving fresh and store the rest in individual single-portion containers in the refrigerator.

Lunch: Prep Italian Wedding Soup with Turkey and Quinoa (page 33) and store the rest in a glass container in the refrigerator.

Dinner: Prep One-Pan Mexican Rice with Chicken (page 108), eat 1 serving fresh and store the rest in a glass container in the fridge for the next day.

Tuesday

Breakfast: Eat 1 serving of prepped Overnight Oats Three Ways (page 168).

Lunch: Eat 1 serving of prepped One-Pan Mexican Rice with Chicken (page 108).

Dinner: Prep Baked Chipotle-Lime Salmon (page 124), dividing the recipe in half to make just 1 portion, and enjoy it freshly made.

Wednesday

Breakfast: Prep Baked Polenta with Spinach and Tofu (page 160), eat 1 serving fresh and store the rest in a glass container in the fridge.

Lunch: Eat 1 serving of prepped Italian Wedding Soup with Turkey and Quinoa (page 33).

Dinner: Prep Stuffed Zucchini Boats with Rice and Chickpeas (page 59), eat 1 serving fresh and store the rest in a glass container in the fridge for the next day.

Thursday

Breakfast: Eat 1 serving of prepped Baked Polenta with Spinach and Tofu (page 160).

Lunch: Eat 1 serving of prepped Stuffed Zucchini Boats with Rice and Chickpeas (page 59).

Dinner: Prep Baked Turkey Meatballs with Mint Yogurt Sauce (page 65), eat 1 serving fresh and store the rest in a glass container in the fridge for the next day.

Friday

Breakfast: Prep Boiled Egg Breakfast Bowl (page 159), eat 1 serving fresh and store the rest in a glass container in the fridge for the next day.

Lunch: Eat 1 serving of prepped Baked Turkey Meatballs with Mint Yogurt Sauce (page 65).

Dinner: Prep Baked Shrimp and Beans (page 111), eat 1 serving fresh and store the rest in a glass container in the fridge for the next day.

Week 3

Meal Plan

Dairy-Free Spanakopita with Tofu and Spinach (page 76)

Spicy Ramen with Broccoli and Mushrooms in Homemade Beef Broth (page 91)

Juicy Baked Chicken Parm (page 42)

Rustic Bolognese with Beef and Eggplant (page 45)

Wholesome Smoothie Blends (page 171)

Grilled Shrimp Tacos with Homemade Salsa (page 120)

Veggie Frittata with Feta (page 153)

Taco Bowl with Roasted Veggies, Quinoa and Beans (page 148)

Bibimbap with Juicy Sirloin, Cucumbers, Shiitake Mushrooms and Carrots (page 88)

Monday

Breakfast: Prep Dairy-Free Spanakopita with Tofu and Spinach (page 76), eat 1 serving fresh and store the rest in a glass container in the fridge for the next day.

Lunch: Prep Spicy Ramen with Broccoli and Mushrooms in Homemade Beef Broth (page 91) and make and eat 1 large serving fresh.

Dinner: Prep Juicy Baked Chicken Parm (page 42), eat 1 serving fresh and store the rest in a glass container in the fridge for the next day.

Tuesday

Breakfast: Eat 1 portion of prepped Dairy-Free Spanakopita with Tofu and Spinach (page 76).

Lunch: Eat 1 portion of prepped Juicy Baked Chicken Parm (page 42).

Dinner: Prep Rustic Bolognese with Beef and Eggplant (page 45), eat 1 serving fresh and store the rest in a glass container in the fridge for the next day.

Wednesday

Breakfast: Pick one Wholesome Smoothie Blend (page 171) and eat 1 serving fresh.

Lunch: Eat 1 serving of prepped Rustic Bolognese with Beef and Eggplant (page 45).

Dinner: Prep Grilled Shrimp Tacos with Homemade Salsa (page 120), eat 1 serving fresh and store the rest in a glass container in the fridge for the next day.

Thursday

Breakfast: Prep Veggie Frittata with Feta (page 153), eat 1 serving fresh and store the rest in a glass container in the fridge for the next day.

Lunch: Eat 1 serving of prepped Grilled Shrimp Tacos with Homemade Salsa (page 120).

Dinner: Prep Taco Bowl with Roasted Veggies, Quinoa and Beans (page 148), eat 1 serving fresh and store the rest in a glass container in the fridge for the next day.

Friday

Breakfast: Eat 1 serving of prepped Veggie Frittata with Feta (page 153).

Lunch: Eat 1 serving of prepped Taco Bowl with Roasted Veggies, Quinoa and Beans (page 148).

Dinner: Prep Bibimbap with Juicy Sirloin, Cucumbers, Shiitake Mushrooms and Carrots (page 88), dividing the recipe in four to make just one portion, and enjoy it freshly made.

Week 4

Meal Plan

Overnight Oats Three Ways (page 168)

Tofu Cabbage Curry (page 84)

Weeknight Taco Skillet with Grass-Fed Beef (page 123)

Baked Polenta with Spinach and Tofu (page 160)

Baked Stuffed Peppers with Ground Turkey and Rice (page 69)

Shrimp and Orange Lover Bowl (page 136)

Wholesome Smoothie Blends (page 171)

Quinoa Galore Bowl with Mediterranean Dressing (page 144)

Gluten-Free High Protein Pancakes with Blueberry Chia Jam (page 154)

Grilled Ahi Tuna Bowl with Edamame, Spiralized Carrots and Cucumbers (page 131)

Monday

Breakfast: Prep Overnight Oats Three Ways (page 168), eat 1 serving fresh and store the rest in individual single-portion containers in the fridge for the next day.

Lunch: Prep Tofu Cabbage Curry (page 84), eat 1 serving fresh and store the rest in a glass container in the fridge for the next day.

Dinner: Prep Weeknight Taco Skillet with Grass-Fed Beef (page 123), eat 1 serving fresh and store the rest in a glass container in the fridge for the next day.

Tuesday

Breakfast: Prep Baked Polenta with Spinach and Tofu (page 160), eat 1 serving fresh and store the rest in a glass container in the fridge.

Lunch: Eat 1 portion of prepped Weeknight Taco Skillet with Grass-Fed Beef (page 123).

Dinner: Prep Baked Stuffed Peppers with Ground Turkey and Rice (page 69), eat 1 serving fresh and store the rest in a glass container in the fridge for the next day.

Wednesday

Breakfast: Eat 1 portion of prepped Baked Polenta with Spinach and Tofu (page 160).

Lunch: Eat 1 serving of prepped Tofu Cabbage Curry (page 84).

Dinner: Prep Shrimp and Orange Lover Bowl (page 136), divide the recipe in half to make just one portion and enjoy it freshly made.

Thursday

Breakfast: Pick one Wholesome Smoothie Blend (page 171) and eat 1 serving fresh.

Lunch: Eat 1 serving of prepped Baked Stuffed Peppers with Ground Turkey and Rice (page 69).

Dinner: Prep Quinoa Galore Bowl with Mediterranean Dressing (page 144), eat 1 serving fresh and store the rest in a glass container in the fridge for the next day.

Friday

Breakfast: Prep Gluten-Free High Protein Pancakes with Blueberry Chia Jam (page 154), dividing the recipe in half to make just one portion, and enjoy it freshly made.

Lunch: Eat 1 serving of prepped Quinoa Galore Bowl with Mediterranean Dressing (page 144).

Dinner: Prep Grilled Ahi Tuna Bowl with Edamame, Spiralized Carrots and Cucumbers (page 131) and eat 1 serving fresh.

Weekend Ready

Any of the weekday recipes you loved you may repeat during the weekends—or you can get creative and freestyle your meals. By the time the weekend comes around, you will be a true pro when it comes to grabbing something out of your fridge and pantry and whipping up a delicious meal.

A lot of the recipes in this meal prep cookbook are family friendly but also great for entertaining. I suggest throwing a Saturday fiesta and serving Grilled Chicken Fajitas with Peppers and Onions (page 113) and Grilled Shrimp Tacos with Homemade Salsa (page 120), along with some rice (page 14).

Or how about an Italian night featuring Two-Ingredient Dough Flatbread Pizza (page 53), Juicy Baked Chicken Parm (page 42) or Hearty Homestyle Meatballs (page 50)?

Feeling like exploring Asian flavors? Cook up Bibimbap with Juicy Sirloin, Cucumbers, Shiitake Mushrooms and Carrots (page 88), Takeout-Style Kung Pao Chicken (page 103) or Baked Teriyaki-Glazed Chicken Wings (page 87).

Feeling nostalgic after a nice summer? How about throwing a Greek-themed party with Not Your Traditional Greek Salad (page 61), Grilled Chicken Gyros with Homemade Gyro Spice (page 72) and Mediterranean Zucchini-Shrimp Salad (page 79)?

Needless to say, you will have plenty to choose from on the weekends as well!

Bella Italia

Italy has always been known for delicious food, but most people associate Italy with pasta and pizza. If you truly dive deeper into Italian culture, you will find that Italians eat way beyond that. Their diet is rich in vegetables, legumes, seafood and meat as well. Inspired by that diet, in this chapter you will find Italian Wedding Soup with Turkey and Quinoa (page 33), High Protein Fagioli Soup with Chickpea Pasta (page 39), Pan-Seared Whitefish Filets in Tomato Sauce (page 40) and Simple Shrimp Risotto with Saffron (page 46). But of course, you will also find some crowd-pleasing and family favorites, such as Juicy Baked Chicken Parm (page 42), Rustic Bolognese with Beef and Eggplant (page 45) and Hearty Homestyle Meatballs (page 50).

Italian Wedding Soup
with Turkey and Quinoa

Yield: 4 servings

This dish is traditionally made with acini di pepe (tiny round pasta) or orzo, but I love making it with quinoa. I like the texture that quinoa gives to this dish, plus you cannot beat the nutritional value! Turkey meatballs make this soup a little lighter than the traditional pork and beef meatballs, yet the end result is a soup that's just as delicious!

Ingredients

½ lb (227 g) ground turkey

1 egg

3 tbsp (45 ml) olive oil, divided

Olive oil or avocado oil spray

1 yellow onion, chopped

1 parsnip, chopped

1 medium carrot, chopped

1 tbsp (4 g) fresh parsley, chopped

1 tsp dried basil

1 tbsp (4 g) fresh oregano, chopped

2 tsp Himalayan salt

¼ tsp crushed red pepper, optional

Black pepper to taste

2 bunches collard greens or 3 handfuls spinach, roughly chopped

½ cup (85 g) uncooked quinoa

4 tbsp (60 ml) tomato puree

8 cups (1920 ml) water

Cooking Method

Place the ground turkey in a mixing bowl, then add in the egg. Mix it by using a wooden spoon or by using your hands until the egg is incorporated.

Add 2 tablespoons (30 ml) of olive oil to a large nonstick pan. When it's warm, scoop some of the meat with a teaspoon and drop it in the pan to form tiny meatballs. Flip them on the other side after about 30 seconds. Once they are done, about 5 minutes, scoop out the meatballs with a slotted spoon and set them aside.

Alternatively, you can use an air fryer. Place the meatballs in the air fryer, spray them with olive or avocado oil and then air fry them for about 6 minutes at 400°F (200°C).

In the same pan, add another tablespoon (15 ml) of olive oil, then add in the onion, parsnip, carrot and parsley. Sauté them for about 2 minutes, then add in the basil, oregano, salt, red pepper and black pepper. Stir the mixture well, then add the meatballs back in along with the collard greens and uncooked quinoa. Add the tomato puree and water, cover the pan and cook the soup over medium heat for about 25 minutes. If you'd like the soup to be thicker, cook it with the lid off for the last 5 minutes.

Meal Prep Notes

For an extra dose of deliciousness, serve the soup with a slice of toasted Gluten-Free Homemade Bread with Buckwheat, Oat and Sesame (page 167).

Split the soup into single servings, and store it in glass containers in the fridge over the next 4 days or freeze it for up to 3 months.

White Bean and Roasted Red Pepper Salad

Yield: 4–6 servings

Roasted red peppers and white butter beans are so wonderful together, especially when combined with olives. This dish is very filling due to the high amount of protein and fiber in beans as well as the good fats in olives and, of course, olive oil. Red wine vinegar adds a perfect touch of acidity to offset the sweetness of the roasted peppers and shallots.

Ingredients

1 cup roasted (150 g) red peppers, chopped (page 9)

2 (15-oz [425-g]) cans white butter beans, drained

½ cup (90 g) kalamata olives

1 shallot, sliced thinly

2 tsp oregano

½ tsp–¾ tsp Himalayan salt

2 tbsp (30 ml) olive oil

2 tbsp (30 ml) red or white wine vinegar

Prep Ahead

Prepare the roasted red peppers as described in the Colorful, Nutrient-Dense Veggies section (page 9).

Cooking Method

Drain and rinse the beans, then add them to a large mixing bowl. Add the olives and shallot as well as the prepared roasted red peppers. Stir them gently, then add the oregano, salt, olive oil and vinegar. Lightly toss the ingredients to combine them.

*See full photo on page 30.

Meal Prep Notes

Store the bean salad in a glass storage container in the fridge over the next 5 days.

This salad goes wonderfully as a side dish for the Pan-Seared Whitefish Filets in Tomato Sauce (page 40) as well as Juicy Baked Chicken Parm (page 42).

Vegetarian Lasagna
with Tofu, Spinach and Ricotta

Yield: 4–6 servings

I absolutely love lasagna, but the traditional versions, although delicious, always leave me with a really heavy feeling in my stomach. Perhaps it's the cheese in combination with béchamel sauce, which is basically a mixture of milk and flour. As with any dish that I like, I had to find a way to healthify it and make it a little more nutritious.

My two favorite ways to make a healthier version of lasagna are to use ground turkey or to make a plant-based version with tofu. I use ricotta cheese in both versions, as this cheese is much lighter in nature than mozzarella. In this vegetarian version, I wanted to add some more vegetables, so I opted for fresh spinach, although collard greens would also work well.

Ingredients

7 cups (210 g) baby spinach (about 1 cup [225 g] cooked)

1 cup (246 g) ricotta cheese

7 oz (200 g) silken or regular tofu, crumbled

1 tsp Himalayan salt

¾ tsp garlic powder

½ tsp thyme

¾ tsp basil

2 (15-oz [425-g]) cans crushed tomatoes

8 oven-ready lasagna sheets

2 tbsp (14 g) part-skim shredded mozzarella cheese

1 tsp dried basil or 2 tbsp (5 g) chopped fresh basil

Prep Ahead

Add the spinach to a small saucepan and cover it with water. Boil for it about 3 minutes, then remove the pan from the heat and drain it through a strainer. Allow the spinach to cool down to room temperature.

Meanwhile, in a mixing bowl, add the ricotta and crumbled tofu along with the salt, garlic powder, thyme and basil and mix them well. Once the spinach has cooled down, add it to the ricotta mixture and stir to combine them.

You can use this prepared spinach, tofu and ricotta mixture right away or store it in a glass container in the fridge for later use.

(Continued)

Vegetarian Lasagna (Continued)

Cooking Method

Preheat the oven to 400°F (200°C). Line a small 9 x 6–inch (23 x 15–cm) baking pan with parchment paper.

Before you start assembling the lasagna, divide the ricotta mixture into three parts and the crushed tomatoes into four parts.

Start by placing two lasagna sheets on the bottom of the baking pan. Spread the first portion of the ricotta mixture, then add a portion of crushed tomatoes. Repeat those steps two more times.

The last layer on the lasagna will be the sheets with just tomatoes on top. Add the shredded mozzarella cheese and dried basil. If using fresh basil, do not add it before baking; add it once you take the lasagna out of the oven.

Bake the lasagna for about 20 to 25 minutes. If you like to get a crispy top, you can turn on the broil setting for the last 3 minutes. Once you take the lasagna out of the oven, cut it into six squares right away and then let it rest for a few minutes before serving.

Meal Prep Notes

To serve, add two pieces of lasagna to each plate along with some fresh greens. My favorite accompaniment is a garden salad with arugula, cherry tomatoes and parmesan cheese, with some olive oil and lemon. Another option I love is a shredded cabbage salad, also with olive oil and lemon.

You can place leftovers in a glass container and store them in the fridge over the next 3 days.

This lasagna can also be fully assembled and stored in the fridge overnight. The next day, you can just stick it in the oven for an easy, hassle-free meal!

High Protein Fagioli Soup
with Chickpea Pasta

Yield: 6 cups cooked (3 servings)

Soups that are hearty, such as this one, are not only delicious but are also nutritionally dense. High protein and high fiber ingredients such as beans and chickpea pasta make this soup really filling, and that is something we should strive for when we plan our meals. I usually suggest this type of soup for lunch or as a dinner add-on, but you can also have it in between meals. Who says soup can't be a good snack? I say go for it, especially during colder months of the year. And for an even more filling meal, add a slice of toasted Gluten-Free Homemade Bread with Buckwheat, Oat and Sesame (page 167).

Ingredients

1 small onion

1 medium carrot

1 celery rib or small parsnip

1 tbsp (4 g) fresh parsley (optional)

2 tbsp (30 ml) olive oil

2–3 tsp Himalayan salt

1 tsp oregano

1 tsp basil

1 tsp garlic powder

½ green zucchini, diced

1 (14.5-oz [410-g]) can whole tomatoes

6 cups (1440 ml) water

1 (15-oz [425-g]) can beans, cannellini or white, drained and rinsed

2 cups (150 g) chickpea fusilli pasta

Prep Ahead

Finely dice the onion, carrot and celery. Chop the parsley and store them all together in a Ziploc® bag in the fridge for up to 3 days. Alternatively, you can dice them and store them each separately in small glass jars to use as needed over the next 5 days.

Cooking Method

In a large soup pot, heat the olive oil and add the onion, carrot, celery and parsley. Sauté them until the onion softens, about 1 minute, then add the salt, oregano, basil and garlic powder. Stir them well, then add the zucchini, tomatoes and water. Cover the pot and bring the soup to a boil over high heat. Once it's boiling, reduce the heat to a simmer and cook for 10 minutes. Add the beans and chickpea pasta, then cover the pot again and continue cooking for about 15 minutes or until the pasta is cooked through.

Meal Prep Notes

Enjoy one serving of the soup and allow the rest to cool down. Once it has cooled, portion it into two containers or jars. Store the soup in the fridge for up to 5 days or in the freezer for up to 3 months.

When you are ready to have it the next day, warm it up on the stove or in the microwave. If the soup is frozen, allow it to defrost at room temperature overnight and then warm it up.

Pan-Seared Whitefish Filets

in Tomato Sauce

Yield: 2 servings

To me, this is one of the best ways to prepare fish so that it can be eaten even the next day without compromising the taste. The fish is cooked in tomato sauce, and then overnight the sauce actually marinates the fish even further, so the next day when warmed up, the flavor is even more developed.

For this recipe, it is best to use firm whitefish filets that are at least 1 inch in thickness, as they will cook more nicely in the tomato sauce and won't fall apart. Some good choices would be cod, mahi mahi, halibut and snapper.

Ingredients

2 tbsp (30 ml) olive oil, divided

1 shallot, minced

1 clove garlic, chopped

1 (15-oz [425-g]) can San Marzano crushed tomatoes

1 tsp basil

¾–1 tsp Himalayan salt

13 oz (364 g) whitefish filets of your choice

1 tbsp (3 g) fresh chives, minced

1 tbsp (15 g) capers

Cooking Method

Add 1 tablespoon (15 ml) of olive oil to a medium size pan with a lid, over medium heat. When the oil is warm, add the shallot in. Sauté the shallot for about 1 minute, then add the garlic, crushed tomatoes, basil and salt. Cover the pan and cook the sauce over medium to low heat for about 10 minutes.

Add the fish filets to the pan along with 1 tablespoon (15 ml) of olive oil, then cover the pan and let it simmer for the next 10 minutes. Add the chives and capers and cook, uncovered, for another couple of minutes, or until the tomato sauce seems unified and not watery anymore.

Meal Prep Notes

Plate one serving of the fish along with some rice (page 14) and one serving of Mediterranean Green Lentil Salad Bowl (page 139). Alternatively, serve it with White Bean and Roasted Red Pepper Salad (page 34).

Any leftover fish can be placed in a storage container and put into the fridge after it has cooled down completely. Fish is best eaten fresh or the following day.

Juicy Baked Chicken Parm

Yield: 8 servings

This dish is a little complex to make, but boy is it worth it! Even though there are a few steps to this dish, preparing some parts ahead really speeds up the process. Marinating the chicken the night before helps it to not dry out while it is baking. Seasoned bread crumbs add a special touch to this dish, and fresh herbs do as well.

Here are some recipes that I suggest you pair the baked chicken parm with: Not Your Traditional Greek Salad (page 61), Grilled Zucchini with Red Onion–Rosemary Marinade (page 75), Rice and Lentils with Caramelized Onions (page 119), Mediterranean Green Lentil Salad Bowl (page 139), Grilled Halloumi Couscous Bowl (page 147) and Quinoa Galore Bowl with Mediterranean Dressing (page 144).

Ingredients

1¾ lb (800 g) chicken breast, sliced thin (about 8 thin slices)

1¼ tsp Himalayan salt, divided

2 tbsp (30 ml) olive oil, plus more for drizzling

1 lemon, squeezed

½ cup (54 g) gluten-free bread crumbs

¼ tsp garlic powder

¼ tsp oregano

¼ tsp dried basil

½ cup (60 g) flour of choice (whole wheat, almond, rice, einkorn)

2 eggs, beaten

Olive oil spray

1 (14-oz [400-g]) jar marinara or arrabbiata sauce

9 oz (250 g) fresh mozzarella cheese, sliced thin

4 tsp grated parmesan cheese

A few tbsp (8 g) fresh basil, chopped

Prep Ahead

Add the chicken breast slices to a container with a cover along with 1 teaspoon of salt, 2 tablespoons (30 ml) of olive oil and the lemon juice. Mix it well and refrigerate it overnight or for at least 30 minutes.

To prepare the bread crumbs, in a container with a lid, mix the bread crumbs, garlic powder, oregano, basil and ¼ teaspoon of salt. Store them with the lid on until you're ready to use them.

Cooking Method

Cover a large baking sheet with parchment paper. Preheat the oven to 400°F (200°C).

Prepare three soup bowls and add the flour in one, the beaten eggs in the second and the seasoned bread crumbs in the third. Take the chicken slices and cover the cutlets in flour first, then the egg and finally the bread crumbs. Place the cutlets on the baking sheet and spray each one with some olive oil.

On each chicken cutlet, add 1 to 2 tablespoons (15 to 30 ml) of marinara sauce, then 1 slice of mozzarella and some parmesan (about ½ teaspoon per cutlet). Bake the chicken for about 25 minutes or until the cutlets are browned and the mozzarella melted. Once you take the chicken out of the oven, add some fresh basil on top and a drizzle of olive oil.

Meal Prep Notes

When you're ready to serve it, place the chicken in the oven to warm it or use the stove top and heat it up in an egg pan. Drizzle a little olive oil on the bottom of the pan, add the chicken along with 1 tablespoon (15 ml) of water and cover it with a lid. The water will warm up the chicken while ensuring it will not dry out.

Rustic Bolognese
with Beef and Eggplant

Yield: 4 servings

This is probably one of my favorite dishes to meal prep because it can be transformed in so many different ways in the days after you make it. The first day you can serve it with zoodles (page 9), the second day with whole grain spaghetti and the third day you can use the sauce to make burritos—just add some plain rice (page 14) and some iceberg lettuce or arugula.

This version of Bolognese uses ground beef, but feel free to use ground veal or ground turkey for a lighter version of the dish.

Meal Prep Notes

Bolognese stores really well. When stored in the fridge, it can stay fresh for up to a week and in the freezer for up to 3 months. To store it, allow the sauce to cool, then transfer it to storage containers and place them in the fridge or freezer.

Ingredients

2 tbsp (30 ml) olive oil

1 small carrot, grated or minced

1 small celery stalk, minced

1 yellow onion, cubed

2 cloves garlic, minced

½ small eggplant or zucchini, grated

1 lb 3 oz (540 g) ground beef

3 cups (720 ml) tomato puree

1½ cups (360 ml) water

1 tsp Himalayan salt

1 tsp oregano

1 tsp basil

Black pepper to taste

Cooking Method

Add the olive oil to a large pan and when it's warm, add the carrot, celery, onion and garlic. Sauté for about 2 minutes, then add the eggplant in as well as the ground beef. After the meat browns, or about 5 minutes, add the tomato puree, water, salt, oregano and basil. Lower the heat to medium-low, cover the sauce and cook it for about 40 to 45 minutes. Add black pepper to taste.

Simple Shrimp Risotto
with Saffron

Yield: 4–6 servings

Would you like to know the secret to a perfectly creamy risotto? You might think it's adding butter, but it's not. The secret is cooking the risotto on a low temperature and adding boiled water or seafood stock in small amounts. So a little patience does wonders when it comes to the creaminess of the risotto! But do not fret: Rice cooks rather fast, so your perfectly cooked risotto will be ready in about 20 minutes or so.

When asparagus is in season, I like to use it in this recipe instead of shrimp. Simply take a bunch of asparagus and steam it for 2 minutes. Chop it and add it toward the end of the cooking time, just like we add the shrimp in the recipe. The spices stay the same—saffron is wonderful in this combination as well. Add a little shredded parmesan at the end, and voilà!

Ingredients

3½ cups (840 ml) water or seafood stock

4 tbsp (60 ml) olive oil

1 large yellow onion, chopped

3 cloves garlic, minced

1½ cups (300 g) uncooked Arborio rice

½ tsp saffron (about two pinches)

1 tsp Himalayan salt

1 lb (454 g) shrimp

Cooking Method

In a small saucepan, add the water or stock and bring it to a boil. Once it's boiling, turn off the heat and set the water aside to use during the cooking process.

Add the olive oil to a large wide pot with a lid (it's best to use something with a thick bottom). Add the onion and garlic and stir until the onion is translucent. Add the rice in, then the saffron and salt. Stir for about 2 minutes, then add 1½ cups (360 ml) of the boiled water.

Cover the pot and cook the risotto for about 5 minutes. Once the water has almost evaporated, add another ½ cup (120 ml). Cover again and cook for another 5 minutes or so.

Add the shrimp and the rest of the warm liquid (you will have about 1½ cups [360 ml] left). Cover it and cook until the risotto unifies and the shrimp is cooked through, about 6 minutes depending on the size of the shrimp you use.

Meal Prep Notes

Shrimp risotto stores really well in the fridge, but it's best if used in 1 to 2 days. Serve one portion fresh, along with a nice large garden salad with mixed lettuce greens and some olive oil and lemon. Allow the rest to cool down, then transfer the risotto to a storage container and place it in the fridge.

To warm up, use a small nonstick pan and add just a few tablespoons of water so you can stir the risotto. Alternatively, you may warm it up in the microwave.

Spicy Shrimp Zoodles
with Hearty Marinara Sauce

Yield: 2 servings

This is one perfect, light summer dish, but it can certainly be on the menu all year round. The sauce is so versatile and can be used with any pasta or even as a lasagna sauce. If you don't like the chunky texture of the sauce, you can always blend it after it's made.

This homemade marinara sauce is a great alternative to the store-bought ones because it doesn't contain any added sugars. And if you make a big batch and store it in the fridge, it becomes just as convenient.

Ingredients

Marinara Sauce
3 tbsp (45 ml) olive oil, divided
1 small leek, sliced thin
¼ red onion, sliced thin
3 cloves garlic, minced
1 (15-oz [425-g]) can crushed tomatoes
1 cup (240 ml) water
½ tsp oregano
½ tsp basil
1 tsp salt
¼ tsp red pepper flakes

Shrimp Zoodles
1 lb (454 g) shrimp
2 large zucchini, spiralized (page 9)
1 tbsp (15 ml) olive oil, or olive oil spray
1 tbsp (3 g) fresh basil, chopped (optional)
Black pepper to taste (optional)

Prep Ahead

Heat 2 tablespoons (30 ml) of olive oil in a medium size pan and add the leek, onion and garlic. Sauté the veggies for about 2 minutes, then add the crushed tomatoes, water, oregano, basil, salt and red pepper flakes.

Cover and cook for about 20 to 25 minutes over medium-low heat. If you aren't using the sauce right away, allow it to cool, then transfer it to a storage container and refrigerate it overnight. The next day, warm it up on the stove.

Cooking Method

To prepare the shrimp, spray the grill pan with some olive oil, place the shrimp and panfry them for 1½ to 2 minutes on one side. Flip and fry for another 1½ to 2 minutes. The shrimp will become opaque and very light pink in color. Transfer the shrimp to the already warm marinara sauce and cover it with a lid.

Meanwhile, preheat the oven to 425°F (220°C). Line a sheet pan with parchment paper, then add the zoodles. Toss the zoodles with olive oil or spray them with olive oil spray and bake them for about 10 minutes. The zoodles should be tender to the touch when you test them with a fork.

Transfer the zoodles onto two plates. If not using both servings, add one serving to a plate and the other one to a glass storage container. On each of the servings, ladle the marinara sauce with shrimp. Sprinkle some freshly chopped basil and black pepper on top if desired.

Meal Prep Notes

Marinara sauce and zoodles store really well in the fridge for up to 5 days. To serve this dish, add the zoodles to the marinara and warm them up in the same pan.

Hearty Homestyle Meatballs

Yield: 5–6 servings

Meatballs must be one of my favorite Italian dishes to make! The best thing about this dish is that it can be made and served many different ways. For a lighter version, use ground turkey and serve over zoodles (page 9); for more of a traditional version, use three types of meat—beef, pork and veal—and serve them over whole grain spaghetti, just like in the recipe below. Using the three types of meat really makes these meatballs extra juicy and flavorful. And if you would like to sneak in some veggies, feel free to grate in one small zucchini instead of adding water in the recipe. This also makes the meatballs extra juicy, and no one will ever know you added a veggie in.

Meatballs make a great meal prep dish because they are delicious when warmed up. In fact, they taste as if you just cooked them.

Ingredients

1 lb (454 g) ground beef

½ lb (226 g) ground pork

½ lb (226 g) ground veal

1 yellow onion, chopped

2 cloves garlic, minced

¼ cup (27 g) whole wheat bread crumbs

1 tbsp (4 g) chopped fresh parsley

1 tsp dried basil

1 tsp garlic powder

2 tsp Himalayan salt, divided

1 egg

¼ cup (60 ml) warm water

1–2 tbsp (15–30 ml) olive oil for basting the pan

5 cups (1200 ml) tomato puree

1½ cups (360 ml) water

1 tsp dried or 1 tbsp (4 g) fresh oregano

Black pepper to taste

(Continued)

Hearty Homestyle Meatballs (Continued)

Prep Ahead

Place the ground beef, pork and veal in a large mixing bowl, followed by the onion, garlic, bread crumbs, parsley, basil, garlic powder and 1 teaspoon of salt. Mix it well by using your hands, then add the egg and warm water and continue mixing with a fork until everything is unified. Form small meatballs and place them on a plate.

If you are cooking the meatballs right away, proceed as described below. If you are storing the meatballs in the fridge to prepare the next day, place them in a large container with a lid and store them in the fridge overnight.

Alternatively, you may separate the meatballs into single and double servings in a Ziploc® bag and freeze them for later use. Meatballs can stay fresh in the freezer like this for up to a month.

Cooking Method

Add the olive oil to a large nonstick pan and when it's warm, add the meatballs in. Lightly panfry them until the meatballs are browned on all sides and no longer pink inside. You may need to do this in a few batches.

Alternatively, you may fry the meatballs in an air fryer at 400°F (200°C) for about 6 minutes (flipping them halfway through frying). Then proceed with cooking as described below.

Take out the meatballs with a slotted spoon, then scrape the bottom of the pan and add the tomato puree, water, 1 teaspoon of salt, oregano and black pepper. Stir to combine them and, once you bring the sauce to a boil, add the meatballs back in one by one. Gently scoop some tomato sauce over each of the meatballs until they are all coated nicely. Cover the pan with a lid, lower the heat and cook for about 40 minutes.

Meal Prep Notes

Enjoy one serving of the meatballs with some quinoa (page 13), rice (page 14) or zoodles (page 9). Allow the rest of the meatballs to cool down, then split them into single servings and place them in containers with lids. You may store them in the fridge over the next 4 days or freeze them for up to 1 month.

To heat up the meatballs, you can use the stove top. If they are frozen, allow them to defrost overnight in the fridge, then warm them up as you usually would.

I suggest that you make the meatballs with zoodles or whole grain pasta the first day and on the second day serve them with Stuffed Zucchini Boats with Rice and Chickpeas (page 59). And if you are feeling adventurous, add meatballs to a whole grain pita bread with some arugula for the yummiest meatball sub!

Two-Ingredient Dough Flatbread Pizza

Yield: 6 small flatbreads/pizzas (6 servings)

Having frozen pizza dough or flatbread really comes in handy. This particular recipe can be transformed into a few very different meal options. And it's made from only two main ingredients: yogurt and flour!

Feel like having pizza? Top it with your favorite toppings and bake it for just a few minutes, as the crust is already baked. Need a good sandwich to bring to work or school? Take the flatbread out of the freezer and defrost it overnight. Cut it in half, then top it with your favorite sandwich toppings, such as cream cheese, tomatoes, avocado and arugula. Ran out of bread but crave a piece of toast? Take the flatbread out of the freezer and let it sit at room temperature while you get ready in the morning. Cut the flatbread into smaller slices that fit into your toaster and toast them. Add some peanut or almond butter on top along with some bananas and honey. No matter how you prepare it, you will love this easy-to-make flatbread!

Ingredients

Pizza Dough

14 oz (400 g) Greek yogurt (at least 2% fat)

3 cups (375 g) spelt flour or any flour of your choice, plus extra for dusting the pan

1 tsp oregano

1 tsp basil

1 tsp Himalayan salt

½ tsp baking powder

½ tsp baking soda

Pizza Toppings (for one serving)

½ cup (120 ml) tomato puree, pizza sauce or marinara sauce

⅓ cup (37 g) part-skim mozzarella cheese, shredded, or 1 medium round (approx. 125 g) fresh mozzarella, sliced

2 mushrooms, sliced

¼ tsp oregano

1 handful arugula or microgreens of your choice (add these fresh, after baking)

Olive oil, to drizzle

Red pepper flakes (optional)

(Continued)

Two-Ingredient Dough Flatbread Pizza (Continued)

Prep Ahead

Preheat the oven to 400°F (200°C). Line a baking sheet with parchment paper and set it aside.

In a large mixing bowl, add the yogurt, flour, oregano, basil, salt, baking powder and baking soda. Knead the dough until it's unified, about 3 minutes.

Add a few tablespoons of flour to a baking sheet and transfer the dough over. Knead the dough just enough so that it doesn't stick, then stretch it with your hands to form a large rectangle. The dough should be as thin as you can stretch it. Transfer the dough to your lined baking sheet.

Place it in the oven and bake it for about 10 minutes. Take the crust out of the oven and peel it off the baking sheet. If the bottom is not crispy, place the crust with the bottom up for another 3 minutes. If you are making the pizza right away, proceed with cooking as described to the right.

If preparing the crust ahead of time, take it out and let it cool completely on a wire rack. Cut the flatbread with scissors into six individual servings and place them in Ziploc® bags. Freeze for up to 3 months. The crust doesn't need to be defrosted before baking (see the cooking instructions at right).

Cooking Method

If you're using a freshly baked crust, add the tomato puree, mozzarella, mushrooms and oregano. Bake at 425°F (220°C) until the cheese melts. Add the arugula and olive oil, and the red pepper flakes if you are using them. Serve it warm.

If you're using frozen flatbread, just add the toppings on the frozen crust and bake it at 400°F (200°C) for about 10 to 12 minutes or until the cheese melts.

Meal Prep Notes

The pizza can be fully made then stored in the fridge overnight. Just omit the arugula until the next day. Once you are ready to eat the pizza, just pop it in the oven on the convection bake setting and let it crisp up. Add arugula and olive oil and enjoy as if you just baked it fresh!

It's All Greek to Me

A lot of dishes I grew up with stem from Greek or Turkish roots, so Mediterranean flavors have always been very familiar to me. Experimenting with some basic spices and ingredients that are commonly used in Greek dishes—such as oregano, garlic, mint, olive oil and lemon—can transform a dish from very plain to super delicious! In this chapter you will find Greek staple dishes but with my take on them. From Not Your Traditional Greek Salad (page 61) and Dairy-Free Spanakopita with Tofu and Spinach (page 76) to Moussaka with Ground Turkey, Zucchini and Potatoes (page 66) to Baked Stuffed Peppers with Ground Turkey and Rice (page 69), you sure are in for a treat!

Stuffed Zucchini Boats
with Rice and Chickpeas

Yield: 2 servings

Zucchini is one of those great, very neutral vegetables that can go well with almost anything.

Over the years I developed this recipe with the idea to make it plant based but very filling. By using chickpeas, I did exactly that. Nourishing, filling and very delicious! The great thing about this recipe is that the zucchini and rice mixture can be prepared ahead of time. So the next day, all you need to do is put it together and bake it.

I often use leftover Bolognese sauce and zucchini halves to create a brand-new dish out of something I already have on hand. Just prepare and bake the zucchini as described below, but instead of rice and chickpeas, you can add Rustic Bolognese with Beef and Eggplant (see page 45 for the most delicious recipe) and parmesan cheese or mozzarella on top. Bake it until the cheese melts and enjoy it warm. It's a must-try!

Ingredients

1 cup (186 g) cooked rice (page 14)

2 green zucchini

Olive oil spray

½ cup (82 g) cooked chickpeas, rinsed and drained

7½ oz (212 g) arrabbiata sauce or any ready-made sauce, like marinara

½ tsp Himalayan salt

1 tsp basil

1 tsp oregano

Parmesan cheese, if desired

Prep Ahead

Cook the rice as described in the Meal Prep 101 section of the book (page 14). You will only need 1 cup (186 g) for this recipe, so either quarter the Basic White Rice recipe or prepare the full recipe and use the leftover rice for other meals during the week.

(Continued)

Stuffed Zucchini Boats (Continued)

Cooking Method

Preheat the oven to 400°F (200°C).

Cut the zucchini lengthwise and spray it with olive oil. Place it cut side down on the baking pan and then bake it for about 15 minutes or until tender so that a fork can go through it easily. Once the zucchini is baked, take a tablespoon and scoop out the middle of the zucchini. Set it aside to use in the stuffing.

In a mixing bowl, add the rice, chickpeas, about 4 tablespoons (44 g) of the saved zucchini and enough arrabbiata sauce to make everything come together nicely (about 4 tablespoons [60 ml]). Add in the salt, basil and oregano.

Stuff the zucchini with the rice mixture, and on each of the zucchini halves add about 1 teaspoon of arrabbiata sauce on top. Grate some parmesan cheese on top if desired, and then spray some olive oil on top.

Place the stuffed zucchini in the oven. Bake at 425°F (220°C) for about 10 to 15 minutes or until you see a nice crisp.

Meal Prep Notes

Serve one serving of stuffed zucchini while it's warm and allow the rest to cool down. Place the remainder of the meal in a glass container and store it in the fridge for the next 3 days. To warm it up, use a nonstick pan with a lid or the microwave.

If you wish to prepare this dish completely in advance, prepare and bake the zucchini as described above. Allow it to cool completely, then add it to a glass container with a lid. You can also prepare the zucchini stuffing ahead of time. If you wish to do that, once you make the rice mixture with rice and chickpeas, allow it to cool down to room temperature and then add it to a glass container with a lid. When you are ready to enjoy your meal the next day, all you need to do is stuff the zucchini boats and pop them in the oven. It's that easy!

Not Your Traditional Greek Salad

Yield: 2 servings as a side dish

Nutritious, delicious and a true crowd-pleaser! The original Greek salad is made with fresh tomatoes, cucumbers, red onions, green peppers, feta cheese and some olive oil. Although I make the original version often, I love adding different veggies (such as celery), herbs (such as parsley), legumes (such as chickpeas) or grains (such as quinoa). Each of these ingredients adds a new flavor as well as a new texture to this wonderful dish. Adding lemon to it as well gives it the acidity that balances all the ingredients really nicely. And to me, lemon and olive oil are such a wonderful way to dress any salad!

Ingredients

2 cups (300 g) cherry tomatoes, sliced in half

½ English cucumber, diced (about 1 cup [150 g])

2 scallions, chopped

½ red onion, sliced thin

2 tbsp (8 g) chopped fresh parsley

⅓ cup (55 g) cooked chickpeas, drained and rinsed

1 tsp Himalayan salt

½ lemon, squeezed

3 tbsp (45 ml) olive oil

½ cup (75 g) feta cheese

Meal Prep Notes

If you are preparing the salad as a side dish, enjoy one serving fresh, place the second serving in a glass container with a lid and store it in the fridge overnight. This salad is a wonderful addition to Grilled Chicken Gyros with Homemade Gyro Spice (page 72).

Prep Ahead

All the vegetables in this salad, as well as the fresh herbs, can be prepared ahead of time. Dice, chop and slice the tomatoes, cucumber, scallions, onion and parsley and add them to a container with a lid.

Always place tomatoes on the bottom of the container, as they tend to let out moisture. You can store the veggies in the fridge for up to 3 days. When you're ready to serve the salad, add the cooked chickpeas, feta, olive oil, lemon and salt, and toss it to combine and enjoy.

Cooking Method

In a large mixing bowl, add the tomatoes, cucumber, scallions, red onion, fresh parsley and cooked chickpeas. Stir to combine them, then sprinkle salt on top and add the lemon juice and olive oil. Gently toss the salad, then add feta cheese on top.

*See full image on page 56.

Hearty Bean Stew

Yield: 4 servings as a side dish, 2 servings as a main dish

Soups are a great way to add more fiber to your diet. Grains and legumes are the biggest stars when it comes to fiber, but some veggies such as broccoli, cauliflower, kale, endive, carrots, collard greens and beets are great counterparts as well.

Soups can be made in big batches and stored in the fridge or freezer for a really long time, especially if they are made without meat. Storing the soup in single-serving containers can come in really handy when you need to grab lunch and run off to school or work.

This bean soup is very filling as beans are rich not only in fiber but also protein. If you eat this soup as a main dish, one serving will provide you with 24 grams of protein just from the beans. Talk about a powerhouse plant-based nutrient!

Ingredients

1 tbsp (15 ml) olive oil

½ yellow onion, chopped

¼ cup (25 g) celery, chopped

1 (14-oz [400-g]) can red kidney beans, drained and rinsed

½ cup (90 g) canned chopped tomatoes

3 cups (720 ml) low-sodium chicken, beef or vegetable broth

1 bay leaf

¾ tsp Himalayan salt

Cooking Method

Add the olive oil to a medium size saucepan. When it's warm, add in the onion and celery. Sauté for about 2 minutes, then add the red kidney beans, chopped tomatoes, chicken broth, bay leaf and salt. Bring the soup to a boil, then cover it, lower the heat to medium-low and cook it for about 25 minutes.

Meal Prep Notes

Enjoy one serving of this dish fresh and allow the rest to cool down. Once cooled, place it in a glass container. You can store the soup in the fridge for up to 5 days. When you are ready to serve it, warm it up on the stove and enjoy. Alternatively, you may freeze the soup and keep it frozen for up to 3 months.

Baked Turkey Meatballs
with Mint Yogurt Sauce

Yield: 21 mini meatballs (3 servings)

Meatballs may be one of my favorites to make and eat. With sauce or without; baked, fried or air fried; however you choose to make them, they are always delicious.

This recipe is inspired by one of our trips to Greece, where we had the juiciest lamb meatballs with tzatziki sauce. The underlying spices were mint and cumin with a hint of coriander and garlic. The traditional tzatziki is made with yogurt, cucumber and dill, but this yogurt sauce was all about fresh mint and lemon.

Recipes in this book that complement the meatballs include Not Your Traditional Greek Salad (page 61), Quinoa Galore Bowl with Mediterranean Dressing (page 144) and Stuffed Zucchini Boats with Rice and Chickpeas (page 59).

Ingredients

Turkey Meatballs

1 lb (454 g) ground turkey
1 tsp red paprika
1 tsp mint
1 tsp cumin
1 tsp garlic powder
¾ tsp Himalayan salt
½ tsp coriander
1 tbsp (2 g) dried parsley
Olive oil spray

Mint Yogurt Sauce

11 oz (310 g) Greek yogurt
½ lemon, squeezed
½ tsp cumin
½ tsp Himalayan salt
2 tbsp (11 g) fresh mint, chopped

Prep Ahead

In a large mixing bowl, add the ground turkey, paprika, mint, cumin, garlic powder, salt, coriander and parsley. Mix them well, then form mini, bite-size meatballs. Place the meatballs in a large storage container with a lid and place it in the fridge.

Add the yogurt and lemon to a mixing bowl and stir until they're combined. Add the cumin, salt and fresh mint. Mix it and place it in a jar with a lid in the fridge overnight.

Cooking Method

Preheat the oven to 425°F (220°C). Line a sheet pan with parchment paper.

Place the meatballs on a baking sheet and spray them with olive oil spray. Bake them for about 16 to 17 minutes. Alternatively, you may bake the meatballs in an air fryer for about 12 minutes.

Serve them fresh from the oven or at room temperature with the mint yogurt sauce you prepared the day before.

Meal Prep Notes

The meatballs can also be baked the day you make them and stored in the fridge overnight. The next day, they are even nice to have cold with the yogurt sauce. You may also warm them up on a grill pan.

Meatballs tend to toughen when stored in the fridge. If you prepare them ahead of time, it's best to bake them the day of as the bake time is less than 20 minutes.

Moussaka

with Ground Turkey, Zucchini and Potatoes

Yield: 6 servings

This must have been one of my favorite dishes growing up. The version I had as a child was just ground pork and potatoes. Once I started making it, I replaced the pork with ground turkey, added the zucchini and a few more spices and also replaced the milk in the egg mixture with Greek yogurt. The end result is the recipe below, which I hope you will love as much as I do!

One of the reasons I love making moussaka is that in one dish we have a healthy dose of vegetables as well as protein and good fats. One-pan dish for the win!

Ingredients

1 large zucchini, sliced (about 2 cups [300 g])

5 tbsp (75 ml) olive oil, divided

4 scallions, chopped (about ¾ cup [36 g])

1 lb (454 g) ground turkey

1 tsp garlic powder

1 tsp red paprika

1 tsp oregano

1 tsp parsley

2 tsp Himalayan salt, divided

2 potatoes, sliced thin (about 3 cups [450 g])

2 tbsp (30 ml) olive oil, divided

1 tsp basil

2 eggs, beaten

1 cup (240 ml) Greek yogurt

Prep Ahead

Cut the zucchini into thin slices and lay them flat on a paper towel. Place a second paper towel on top, then roll it up into a cylinder. Place the wrapped zucchini in a Ziploc® bag and store it in the fridge overnight.

If using it for dinner the same day, you may leave it at room temperature. Ensure that you let the zucchini rest for at least 20 minutes, as the paper towel will soak up any extra water from the zucchini.

Cooking Method

Preheat the oven to 400°F (200°C).

In a medium sized pan, add 3 tablespoons (45 ml) of olive oil and when it's warm, add the scallions in. Sauté the scallions for about 2 minutes, then add the ground turkey in as well as the garlic powder, red paprika, oregano, parsley and 1 teaspoon of salt. Continue sautéing until the turkey is no longer pink (about 5 minutes). Divide the meat into two halves.

Meanwhile, add the sliced potatoes to a mixing bowl along with 1 tablespoon (15 ml) of olive oil and ½ teaspoon of salt. Mix them and set the bowl aside. In another mixing bowl, add the zucchini slices, 1 tablespoon (15 ml) of olive oil, ½ teaspoon of salt, and the basil and toss to combine them. Divide the zucchini and potatoes in half.

(Continued)

Moussaka (Continued)

Now we have come to the fun part: layering! Take a medium size baking tray, about 7 x 11 inches (18 x 28 cm), and start by layering half the potato slices on the bottom. The next layer will be half the meat mixture, then half the zucchini. Repeat with the second half of each of the ingredients. The last layer will be zucchini, but if you prefer, you can swap the zucchini and potatoes so the potatoes are on top. Place the moussaka in the oven.

Add the eggs and Greek yogurt to a mixing bowl and beat them well. About 35 minutes into baking, remove the pan from the oven, pour the egg mixture on top of the moussaka and bake it for another 15 minutes.

Cut the moussaka in six pieces and serve one piece per person. If you wish, you can add a salad with this meal—butter lettuce with some scallions, olive oil and lemon goes so well!

You can allow any leftovers to cool down, then place them in a glass container and store them in the fridge over the next 3 days. To warm them up, place them on a small baking sheet, cover with foil and bake them until warm.

Meal Prep Notes

As I mentioned in the Prep Ahead section, the zucchini can be prepared the day before. The potatoes can be as well: just peel the potatoes, slice them, add the slices to a bowl and add enough water to cover them (this will prevent the potatoes from darkening).

The meat mixture can also be prepared the day before. Cook the meat as per the instructions above, allow it to cool down to room temperature and then cover it and store it in the fridge overnight.

The next day when you are ready to make the moussaka, all you need to do is assemble and bake it!

Baked Stuffed Peppers
with Ground Turkey and Rice

Yield: 5 servings

This is a wonderful, hearty dish that is very filling and nutritious. Typically, dishes tend to taste best the day they are made, but this may be one of those dishes that tastes even better a few days after. Perhaps it takes some time for the flavors of the rice and meat, along with the peppers and tomatoes, to integrate completely.

In this recipe I combine stove top cooking and baking, but you can just cook it on the stove top or just bake it. The cooking or baking time will vary, but as soon as the peppers are tender and you can poke a fork through them, they are ready. Either way it comes out really delicious!

Ingredients

3 tbsp (45 ml) olive oil, divided

1 yellow onion, finely diced

1 small leek, finely chopped

1 lb (454 g) ground turkey

1 tsp parsley

1 tsp basil

1½ tsp Himalayan salt

¾ cup (150 g) uncooked jasmine rice

10 small or 6 large bell peppers (yellow, green, red)

2 large tomatoes, cut into large chunks that will serve as "lids" for the peppers

1 cup (240 ml) tomato puree

1 tsp oregano

1 tsp Himalayan salt

Black pepper to taste

6 cups (1440 ml) water

Prep Ahead

Add 2 tablespoons (30 ml) of olive oil to a large saucepan and when it's warm, add the onion and leek. Sauté them for a couple of minutes and then add the ground turkey, parsley, basil and salt. When the turkey is no longer pink, about 5 minutes, stir in the rice and remove it from the heat. The meat is now ready for stuffing the peppers.

You have two choices: either use the meat right away to stuff the peppers—or allow it to cool down and place it in a storage container in the fridge or freezer for later use. The stuffing will stay fresh for up to a month in the freezer and up to a week in the fridge.

Also, if you wish to make a small batch of stuffed peppers, feel free to store half the stuffing per the instructions above.

Cooking Method

Preheat the oven to 425°F (220°C).

Wash the peppers and take out the stems. You can do that by slowly cutting around the stem with a sharp knife. Once you cut the full circle, pull the stem out along with the seeds.

Add a few tablespoons of the meat and rice mixture to each of the peppers, then use large tomato chunks to close the peppers so that the meat and rice stay put while cooking.

(Continued)

Baked Stuffed Peppers (Continued)

Add 1 tablespoon (15 ml) of olive oil to a large ovenproof pan that you will use for the peppers, and heat it over medium heat. After a few seconds, add the tomato puree, oregano, salt and black pepper. Cook the sauce for about 2 minutes, then add in the peppers, with the tomatoes facing up. Slowly pour the water around the peppers. Using a large spoon or a ladle, pour some of the tomato sauce on top of the peppers.

Bring the sauce to a boil, then cover and lower the heat to medium-low. Cook it for about 20 minutes and then uncover it, place it in the oven and bake it for about 30 minutes. You may turn on the broiler at the end if you wish to crisp up the tops some more.

Meal Prep Notes

If you used large peppers, plate one pepper as a serving, and if you used smaller peppers, use two. Allow the rest of the stuffed peppers to cool down completely, then transfer them to a storage container. The peppers will stay fresh in the fridge over the next 5 days, or you may freeze them for up to a month.

When you wish to warm up the peppers, it is best to place them in a small saucepan and warm them up on the stove.

Grilled Chicken Gyros
with Homemade Gyro Spice

Yield: 5–6 servings

Chicken is one of those very basic foods, but somehow it's not so simple to cook. Many times, it's dry or just plain tasteless. Using a variety of spices, usually any type of Greek, Middle Eastern or Mexican spice blend, is a wonderful way to make chicken more flavorful.

In this recipe we are flavoring the chicken with a combination of aromatic spices such as oregano, garlic powder, cumin, cinnamon, basil and dill. This juicy chicken makes the most delicious lunch or dinner option when paired with Not Your Traditional Greek Salad (page 61).

For more on preparing great, flavorful chicken, see the marinades section (page 16).

Ingredients

Homemade Gyro Spice

1 tbsp (5 g) dried oregano
1 tbsp (5 g) dried basil
1 tbsp (8 g) garlic powder
1 tbsp (7 g) red paprika
½ tbsp (3 g) cumin
½ tbsp (2 g) dill
½ tbsp (6 g) Himalayan salt
1 tsp cinnamon

Chicken Gyros

1¾ lb (800 g) chicken breast, cut into strips
3 tbsp (45 ml) olive oil
Not Your Traditional Greek Salad (page 61)
Whole wheat wrap or whole wheat pita bread (optional)

Prep Ahead

In a mixing bowl, add the oregano, basil, garlic powder, red paprika, cumin, dill, salt and cinnamon. Mix them and store the gyro spice in a spice container with a lid. You can keep this spice in your pantry for a while.

Add the chicken strips to a Ziploc® bag, then add the olive oil and the gyro spice you just prepared. Mix it well, close the bag and store it in the fridge overnight. If you are planning on making the chicken right away, ensure that you marinate it for at least 20 minutes to allow time for the flavors to marinate.

Cooking Method

If the chicken was in the fridge, place it at room temperature for about 10 minutes. Warm up a grill pan or cast-iron skillet and grill the chicken for about 6 to 8 minutes. The chicken will cook fast since it's cut in strips.

Add one serving of the chicken on a plate along with a serving of Not Your Traditional Greek Salad (page 61). Alternatively, you may add a whole wheat wrap or pita pocket to your plate, then add the chicken and some of the Greek salad. Wrap it up and enjoy!

Meal Prep Notes

For leftovers, store everything separately and combine the day of. This way, the chicken can stay fresh for up to 5 days.

To make a whole new dish with this grilled chicken, take 1 whole wheat pita bread and add some shredded iceberg lettuce, slices of tomatoes, cucumbers, grilled chicken and Mint Yogurt Sauce (page 65).

Grilled Zucchini
with Red Onion–Rosemary Marinade

Yield: 2–4 servings

This is hands down one of my favorite zucchini dishes to make when summer comes. We usually grill a whole batch of zucchini, and then I store it in the fridge for up to 5 days. You can read more on zucchini prep at the beginning of the cookbook (page 8).

The marinade is made with rosemary and parsley, but you can use any fresh herbs of your choice. Oregano, thyme, marjoram, dill—they all work. In this recipe it is important to use good-quality olive oil because the marinade is drizzled on top of the grilled zucchini. It truly makes a difference in taste!

This dish is great to serve with Baked Turkey Meatballs with Mint Yogurt Sauce (page 65), Juicy Baked Chicken Parm (page 42) or Grilled Chicken Gyros with Homemade Gyro Spice (page 72). But it is also wonderful when served with a simple protein on the side such as grilled steak, grilled chicken, rotisserie chicken or pan-seared tofu.

Ingredients

Grilled Zucchini

2 small zucchini

1 tsp Himalayan salt

Olive oil spray

4 tbsp (38 g) feta cheese, crumbled (optional)

Red Onion–Rosemary Marinade

½ red onion, minced

1 tbsp (2 g) fresh rosemary, chopped

1 tbsp (4 g) fresh parsley, chopped

2 tbsp (30 ml) white wine vinegar

3 tbsp (45 ml) olive oil

½ tsp Himalayan salt

Prep Ahead

Cut the zucchini in half lengthwise. Take a knife and slice the white flesh of the zucchini halves, first lengthwise, then across. The cuts should be almost to the bottom of the zucchini—that is, almost to the skin. Doing this will help cook the zucchini faster. Sprinkle salt on each of the halves and then spray them with olive oil.

To grill the zucchini, you can use a grill pan or grill, or you can use a standard nonstick pan. It is important for the grill or the pan to be really hot, otherwise the zucchini will stick to it. Place the zucchini white part down and grill it for about 4 minutes on one side, then flip it to the other side and grill it until the zucchini is tender. A fork should go through it easily.

Allow the zucchini to cool down to room temperature. If you are using the zucchini right away, proceed with the recipe as outlined below. If not, transfer the zucchini to a storage container and store it in the fridge for the next 3 days.

Cooking Method

In a small mixing bowl, add the onion, rosemary, parsley, white wine vinegar, olive oil and salt. Place the zucchini on a plate, then pour about 1 tablespoon (15 ml) of the marinade on top of each of the zucchini. Sprinkle some feta on top and enjoy!

Meal Prep Notes

The zucchini can be stored separately from the marinade, or you can store them together. In the latter case, I do not suggest keeping it for longer than a day, as the fresh herbs can get sour because of the vinegar. Placing the zucchini on its own in a storage container will ensure the zucchini stays fresh for at least 3 days.

Dairy-Free Spanakopita
with Tofu and Spinach

Yield: 3 servings

This savory spinach pie is traditionally made in Greece with spinach, eggs and feta cheese, and in Serbia we make it the same way. Perhaps it's the crispy phyllo dough that really makes this dish irresistible!

When I was developing this recipe, I wanted to make it more protein rich and filling so it could serve as a great nutrient-dense meal even if it was served as a standalone dish. In Greece, this pie is served as an appetizer, and in Serbia we would serve it as part of breakfast or dinner.

Ingredients

3 eggs

1 (14-oz [400-g]) package silken or regular tofu

4 oz (113 g) vegan cheese, shredded or crumbled

1 (5-oz [142-g]) bag baby spinach

1 tsp Himalayan salt

½ (1-lb [454-g]) package whole wheat phyllo dough

Olive oil spray

Cooking Method

Preheat the oven to 400°F (200°C). Line a small 9 x 9–inch (23 x 23–cm) baking pan with parchment paper and set it aside.

In a large mixing bowl, add the eggs and beat them for a few seconds. Crumble the tofu and add it to the egg mixture along with the vegan cheese. Stir well until they are incorporated. Add the spinach in as well as the salt. Mix to combine them.

Take one phyllo sheet and place it on the bottom of the baking pan. Spray some olive oil on top, then add one more sheet, then add a quarter of the spinach and egg mixture.

Repeat the steps until you use up all the spinach. The last layer will be a phyllo sheet sprayed with olive oil.

You can also add a few more sheets on top with olive oil in between. It's nice to have that top part a bit thicker, as it gets really crispy.

Place the spanakopita in the oven and bake it for about 40 minutes. When you take it out of the oven, cover it with a clean kitchen towel and let it rest for about 15 minutes.

Meal Prep Notes

Cut the spanakopita in six pieces and serve two pieces as a serving while it's still fresh out of the oven. Place any leftovers in a glass container and store them in the fridge over the next 2 to 3 days.

You do not need to warm up the spinach pie the next day; you can have it cold, straight from the fridge. But if you wish, you can place it in a small pan and into the oven for just about 10 minutes at 400°F (200°C). It will be as crispy as if you'd first baked it!

All the steps before baking in this recipe can be done the day before. Once you put the spanakopita together, cover it with foil and place it in the fridge. The next day, leave it on the counter while you are preheating the oven, then bake it as instructed.

Mediterranean Zucchini–Shrimp Salad

Yield: 2–4 servings

I am not sure if it's the aromatic herbs in this dish or the citrusy shrimp, but this dish reminds me of Greece and the beach so much! This is a perfect summer dish when you crave something hearty but at the same time light. Typically we see zucchini in warm dishes, but here, although cooked, the zucchini is chilled and served cold. Shrimp with a splash of lime juice adds a perfect balance to the sweetness of the zucchini and shallots.

This makes a great side dish at a barbecue. I suggest you serve it in small single-serve cups. It's also great with White Bean and Roasted Red Pepper Salad (page 34) as well as with some plain jasmine or basmati rice (page 14).

Ingredients

2 tbsp (30 ml) olive oil

2 medium zucchini, cubed (about 2 cups [250 g])

1 shallot, sliced thin

1 tsp dried basil

1 tsp oregano

1 tsp garlic powder

1 tsp Himalayan salt

1 lb (454 g) cooked shrimp with the shells on (about 22 shrimp)

1 lime, squeezed

1 tbsp (2 g) fresh basil

Prep Ahead

Add the olive oil to a medium size pan and when it's warm, add in the zucchini and shallot. Sauté it for about 1 minute, then add the basil, oregano, garlic powder and Himalayan salt. Continue sautéing it for another 5 minutes, or until the zucchini is tender.

Allow the zucchini to cool completely, then add it to a storage container with a lid and refrigerate it.

Cooking Method

Peel the shrimp and add it to a mixing bowl. Squeeze the lime on top and toss the shrimp. Take the zucchini out of the fridge and add it to the mixing bowl with the shrimp. Add some fresh basil and toss it once more to combine.

Meal Prep Notes

This makes two lunch or dinner portions, or four servings if served as a side dish. Any leftovers can be stored in a storage container in the fridge over the next 2 days.

Asian-Inspired Favorites

I have always found Asian food to be very comforting. Perhaps it's the warming spices such as ginger, curry and turmeric or the combination of the sweetness of teriyaki sauce and the spiciness of red chili pepper pastes such as gochugaru. Shrimp Fried Rice (page 101) has always been my favorite dish to eat, and when my best friend taught me how to make it the right way, it quickly became a family favorite. Spicy Ramen with Broccoli and Mushrooms in Homemade Beef Broth (page 91) is also among my favorites, and because it's made with homemade beef broth, it truly is healing and soothing. In this chapter I also included two quick recipes for a light lunch or a quick snack: Spring Rolls with Tofu and Peanut Butter Sesame Dressing (page 83) and Tuna Salad Seaweed Wrap (page 98). For meat lovers, be sure to try Bibimbap with Juicy Sirloin, Cucumbers, Shiitake Mushrooms and Carrots (page 88) and Takeout-Style Kung Pao Chicken (page 103).

Spring Rolls
with Tofu and Peanut Butter Sesame Dressing

Yield: 1 serving

This is one of my favorite ways to use up the fresh veggies I have left in the fridge at the end of the week. For the protein, you can use tofu like I did, but you can also use grilled chicken or grilled shrimp, which are also very delicious options.

The peanut butter dressing does not need any special introduction. It is absolutely perfect in this combination. Feel free to try this dressing on your favorite salads as well!

Ingredients

Peanut Butter Sesame Dressing

1 tbsp (15 ml) creamy peanut butter

1 tbsp (15 ml) soy sauce

1 tsp raw honey

6 tbsp (90 ml) water

1 tsp sesame seeds

Spring Rolls

Olive oil or coconut oil spray

½ (14-oz [400-g]) package firm tofu, sliced in thin slices, pressed

3 sheets rice paper

1 cup (30 g) baby spinach

1 cup (70 g) shredded Chinese cabbage or chopped iceberg lettuce

⅓ cup (37 g) shredded carrot

½ red pepper, thinly sliced

Prep Ahead

Add the peanut butter, soy sauce and honey to a mixing bowl. Mix them well, then slowly pour in the water. Stir it well, then add the sesame seeds in.

Cooking Method

To prepare the tofu, spray the olive or coconut oil on a nonstick pan and when it's warm, add the tofu in. Panfry it for about 2 minutes on one side, then flip it and cook for about 2 more minutes. You will know the tofu is ready when it's nicely browned on both sides.

Alternatively, you can use an air fryer to prepare it. Just spray the tofu with coconut oil and air fry it at 400°F (200°C) for about 6 to 8 minutes.

In order to bend the rice paper, you will need to soak it. Fill up a tray with water, one large enough so that the rice paper fits. Place one sheet of rice paper in the water and wait for a few seconds. When you touch the paper it will start to feel sticky. Take the rice paper out of the water and place it on a clean plate or cutting board.

Starting from the edge, add some spinach, cabbage, carrot, pepper and the tofu. Wrap the rice paper like a burrito by rolling it once, closing the edges and finally giving it one more roll to close it up completely. Drizzle some peanut butter dressing on top.

Tofu Cabbage Curry

Yield: 2 servings

A curry is a dish with a sauce seasoned with warming spices, mainly associated with South Asian cuisine. There are two blends of spices that are most commonly used: yellow and red curry. In this dish we are using yellow curry, which is a mix of aromatic spices such as turmeric, cumin, coriander, fenugreek, garlic, salt, bay leaf, lemongrass, cayenne pepper, ginger, mace and cinnamon. You may also want to try the Curried String Beans with Chickpeas (page 94), which uses red curry paste as a spice, for a bit of a different flavor.

I love making curry dishes because they give me the opportunity to use a wide variety of vegetables. Onion and garlic are always the base, and then you can add zucchini, string beans, okra, peppers, cauliflower and truly any other vegetables that you might like. At times I add shrimp as a protein, but I mainly make curry dishes with tofu, chickpeas or just with vegetables.

Ingredients

1 tbsp (15 ml) olive oil

1 tbsp (15 ml) sesame oil

2 shallots, chopped

4 cloves garlic, chopped

3 cups (210 g) shredded cabbage

½ cup (55 g) shredded carrots

7 oz (200 g) firm tofu, pressed and cubed

2 tbsp (13 g) yellow curry spice

1 tsp Himalayan salt

1 tsp Korean chili flakes

1 cup (240 ml) coconut milk

2 servings jasmine rice (page 14)

Cooking Method

Add the olive and sesame oil to a large pan and when the oil is warm, add the shallots and garlic. Sauté for about 1 minute, then add the shredded cabbage and carrots. Continue stirring for another couple of minutes and then add the tofu, curry, salt and Korean chili flakes.

Add the coconut milk and lower the heat to a simmer. Cook the curry for another 5 minutes or until you get a nice unified curry texture.

Meal Prep Notes

Add one serving of Tofu Cabbage Curry to a serving bowl along with one serving of jasmine rice.

Allow the rest of the curry to cool down to room temperature, then add it to a glass storage container along with a leftover serving of rice. Store it in the fridge overnight.

The next day, when you're ready to serve the curry, add it to a pan and warm it up on the stove together with the rice.

The curry will thicken a little bit in the fridge, so you might need to add just a couple tablespoons of water to it while warming it up.

Baked Teriyaki-Glazed Chicken Wings

Yield: 4–6 servings

I often make chicken wings as appetizers when having friends over. They are a true crowd-pleaser and can be made in big batches. Also, it's really nice that you can prep them ahead, then just pop them in the oven and bake them the next day. The recipe below has Asian flair, but you can also make them spicy with some sriracha and honey or just plain with some Himalayan salt and garlic powder.

Ingredients

¼ cup (60 ml) soy sauce

1 tbsp (15 ml) honey

1 tsp dried garlic powder or ½ tsp minced fresh garlic

½ tsp ground ginger or ¼ tsp minced fresh ginger

1 tbsp (9 g) toasted sesame seeds

2 lb (907 g) chicken wings

Olive oil spray

Prep Ahead

Prepare the marinade by placing the soy sauce, honey, garlic, ginger and sesame seeds in a bowl and stirring to combine them. Add the wings to a glass container with a lid, pour the marinade over them and mix well.

You can marinate the wings for up to 2 days, but ensure you marinate them for at least 30 minutes before you make the dish, so the flavors have time to marinate well.

Cooking Method

Preheat the oven to 425°F (220°C). Line a baking tray with parchment paper and set it aside.

Place the marinated wings on the baking tray and spray them with some olive oil. Bake them at 425°F (220°C) for about 15 minutes, then lower the heat to 400°F (200°C) and bake them for an additional 35 minutes. You may turn the broil setting on high at the end if you want to crisp up the wings even more.

You can also use an air fryer for baking by setting the temperature at 400°F (200°C) and baking the wings for about 20 minutes, turning them once halfway through.

Meal Prep Notes

You can serve the wings as an appetizer along with some celery sticks, or as a dinner dish along with some plain jasmine rice (page 14) or the Teriyaki Mushrooms with Purple Cabbage and Brown Rice Bowl (page 129).

To store them, allow the chicken wings to cool, then place them in a glass container with a lid or in a Ziploc® bag and store them in the fridge over the next 3 days.

To warm them up, place the wings on a baking tray and bake them at 425°F (220°C) for about 15 minutes. Alternatively, you may use an air fryer or a microwave to heat them up as well.

Bibimbap
with Juicy Sirloin, Cucumbers, Shiitake Mushrooms and Carrots

Yield: 4 servings

I love going to restaurants and "dissecting" the dishes I am eating. I think Asian foods are probably the hardest for me to figure out as, culturally, the spices we use are very different. Greek and Italian food are much closer to Serbian food, so I can see right through those dishes most of the time. I am always impressed with the variety and quantity of vegetables in Asian dishes. In American culture, meat is always a main ingredient, and starches and vegetables may or may not be there. Same is true for Serbia. In Asian dishes, vegetables are definitely front and center.

This dish can be very versatile. You may use any vegetables of your choice, and you can even use a different type of protein. I tried making this dish with tofu, and it was so delicious! For the warm vegetables, try using broccoli instead of mushrooms, and add some cooked shelled edamame as well. With just these few swaps you get a whole other dish!

Ingredients

Steak Marinade

1½ lb (680 g) rib eye steak or sirloin

1 tbsp (15 ml) soy sauce

1 tbsp (15 ml) Worcester sauce

2 cloves garlic, crushed

2 tbsp (30 ml) olive oil, divided, plus extra to baste the pan

5 cups (400 g) shiitake mushrooms

Chili Sesame Sauce

6 tbsp (90 ml) soy sauce

6 tbsp (90 ml) rice vinegar

3 tbsp (45 ml) gochugaru chili paste

4 tbsp (36 g) sesame seeds

4 tsp honey

4 tbsp (60 ml) toasted sesame oil

Bibimbap Base

4 cups (744 g) cooked rice (page 14)

½ English cucumber, sliced thin

1 cup (110 g) shredded carrots

2 scallions, green parts only, chopped

(Continued)

Bibimbap (Continued)

Prep Ahead

To prepare the meat, place the steak in a Ziploc® bag along with the soy sauce, Worcester sauce, crushed garlic and 1 tablespoon (15 ml) of olive oil. Rub the steak well until it's nicely coated, then place it in the fridge for at least 30 minutes, or up to 3 days.

In a mixing bowl, prepare the sauce by adding the soy sauce, rice vinegar, gochugaru chili paste, sesame seeds, honey and toasted sesame oil. Stir to combine the sauce and set it aside.

Cooking Method

Baste a cast-iron pan with some olive oil and when it's hot, add the meat in. For medium doneness, grill the steak on one side for about 3 minutes, then flip it to the other side for another 3 minutes. The steak will have a nice crust and will be pink on the inside.

When it's done, let the steak rest for few minutes while you prepare the mushrooms.

In the same skillet where you grilled the meat, add 1 tablespoon (15 ml) of olive oil, then add the mushrooms in. Sauté the mushrooms for about 2 minutes, then add 4 tablespoons (60 ml) of the prepared sauce. Stir the mushrooms, cook them for an additional 3 minutes, and set them aside.

To serve the dish, place 1 cup (186 g) of cooked rice in a bowl with one serving of meat, one serving of mushrooms and then fresh cucumber, carrots and scallions. Pour some of the prepared sauce on top.

Meal Prep Notes

In this recipe, you will get four servings of meat and mushrooms as well as four servings of fresh vegetables (cucumbers, carrots and scallions). You may place any leftover servings of meat, mushrooms and rice in storage containers together and allow them to cool down to room temperature, then place them in the fridge.

The fresh veggies can be stored in a Ziploc® bag and put away. When you're ready to serve it the next day, warm up the meat, mushrooms and rice, add the fresh veggies in and enjoy!

If you wish to have the delicious sauce always handy, make a double or triple batch and store it in a glass jar in the fridge. It can last for at least a week in the fridge, sometimes longer.

Spicy Ramen
with Broccoli and Mushrooms in Homemade Beef Broth

Yield: 2 small servings or 1 large serving of ramen, and about 6 cups of beef broth

I am not sure if it's the coziness of the rice noodles, the warm beef broth or the immune-boosting spice ginger, but this dish just warms up my soul!

Both broccoli and mushrooms are high protein and high fiber ingredients that are very filling and add a perfect balance to starchy rice noodles. Although you can use store-bought beef broth for this recipe, I highly suggest you try this one as well.

This broth recipe would be the same if you wished to make chicken broth. Just use chicken thighs and chicken breast, skin on and bone in. Feeling like having chicken noodle soup? Well, you just made the broth! When you strain the broth, save the carrots and chicken, chop them and add them back in. Bring it to a boil and add soup noodles. Cook the noodles according to the instructions on the box, add some fresh parsley on top and enjoy!

Ingredients

Homemade Beef Broth

¾ lb–1 lb (340–454 g) beef short ribs

1 large onion, cut in half

1 large carrot, roughly chopped

2 parsnips, roughly chopped

½ celery root, roughly chopped

1 leek, roughly chopped

2 tsp Himalayan salt

7–8 cups (1680–1920 ml) water

Ramen

3½ cups (840 ml) homemade beef broth

1¼ cups (114 g) fresh broccoli florets

1¼ cups (100 g) sliced fresh shiitake mushrooms

⅓ package (about 3 oz or 85 g) uncooked rice noodles

½ tsp gochugaru chili flakes or red pepper flakes

½ tsp ground ginger

Salt (if needed, as broth is salty)

(Continued)

Spicy Ramen (Continued)

Prep Ahead

In a large stock pot, add the short ribs, onion, carrot, parsnips, celery root, leek and salt. Add as much water as you can fit into the pot, leaving a few finger-widths free at the top so that it doesn't boil over. You should be able to fit at least 7 to 8 cups (1680 to 1920 ml) of water. Cover the pot, bring it to a boil and cook it over low heat for a few hours.

The longer you cook the soup, the more flavorful the broth will be. You may also place all the broth ingredients in a slow cooker and cook it overnight for 6 hours. The flavor is even richer! But the minimum cooking time should be at least 1 hour.

When the broth is cooked, strain the liquid and divide the broth into portions. Allow the broth to cool completely before storing it. You may use a single-serve container or store it in one large container with a lid. Jars are great for this!

The fattier the meat, the more intense the broth will be. You will notice a layer of fat on top of the broth the next morning. Feel free to add some water to dilute it—it will be just as tasty.

Cooking Method

Place the beef broth in a medium size saucepan and bring it to a boil. Lower the heat and add the broccoli, mushrooms and rice noodles.

Add the chili flakes, ginger and salt. Cover the soup, lower the heat to medium-low and cook for about 5 minutes or until the noodles are cooked based on the instructions on the packaging.

Meal Prep Notes

If you wish to have the ramen ready to go in the morning, feel free to make it, cool it down completely, then add it to a jar with a lid. Store it in the fridge overnight.

The next day, the broth will have thickened a bit, so when you're ready to serve it, pour the ramen in a small saucepan, add about ½ cup (120 ml) of water and bring it to a boil. Adjust the salt if needed.

This homemade beef broth is wonderful to use in any recipe that calls for broth. Try adding it to Hearty Bean Stew (page 62), or have a glass of warm beef broth in the colder months of the year. It's wonderful for our gut health and is a great healing elixir.

Curried String Beans

with Chickpeas

Yield: 4 servings

Both string beans and chickpeas are rich in fiber and protein, a true plant-based power-house duo. When it comes to flavors, these two complement each other really nicely. Red curry paste—usually made with ground red chili pepper, garlic, lemongrass, salt, shallot, coriander and lime—adds a deep flavor to this dish. If you would like to tone down the spiciness, you may add some coconut milk toward the end—just about ⅓ cup (80 ml) would do.

This is a great meal prep dish that can be made as a standalone lunch bowl or as an add-on to a meat dish. And of course, it's always a good idea to serve this with some aromatic jasmine or basmati rice (page 14) or quinoa (page 13).

Ingredients

2 tbsp (30 ml) olive oil

2 shallots, sliced

3 cloves garlic, minced

1 lb (454 g) frozen string beans

2 tbsp (30 g) red curry paste

1½ tsp Himalayan salt

1 (15-oz [425-g]) can chickpeas, rinsed and drained

½ (15-oz [425-g]) can crushed tomatoes

2 cups (480 ml) water

½–1 tsp red chili flakes

Cooking Method

Add the olive oil to a medium size stock pot. When it's warm, add the shallots and garlic. Sauté them for about 1 minute, then add the string beans, curry paste and salt.

Cook the string beans for another minute, then add the chickpeas, crushed tomatoes, water and red chili flakes.

Cover the pot and cook over medium heat for about 25 to 30 minutes.

Meal Prep Notes

Add one serving of the string beans to a bowl to enjoy them fresh and allow the rest to cool down. You can use one large container to store the rest of the string beans, or you can store single portions of string beans along with some rice in single-serve meal prep containers.

The next day, when you're ready to serve the beans, just warm them up in a small saucepan. You can keep them fresh in the fridge over the next 5 days or freeze them for up to a month.

Miso-Glazed Tofu Wrap

Yield: 1–2 servings

When you need a super fast, delicious and nutritious lunch, I suggest you try this tofu wrap recipe. You can use any fresh veggies of your choice for the filling. I like using the crispy kinds such as iceberg lettuce, cabbage and carrots, with avocado for its creaminess. Cucumber and celery are also great, as well as microgreens and arugula. The miso dressing is very versatile: It can be used as a salad dressing but also makes a great marinade for the tofu.

Ingredients

Miso Dressing

2 tbsp (30 g) miso paste
2 tbsp (30 ml) rice vinegar
2 tbsp (30 ml) sesame oil
16 tbsp (240 ml) water
2 tbsp (18 g) sesame seeds

Tofu Wrap

½ (14-oz [400-g]) package firm tofu, cubed, pressed
1 cup (67 g) shredded iceberg lettuce
½ cup (55 g) shredded carrots
½ cup (35 g) shredded purple cabbage
Olive oil spray
2 small whole grain or almond flour tortillas

Meal Prep Notes

If you are having only one wrap, you can mix the remaining prepared tofu with the veggies and place them in a storage container with a lid in the fridge. The next day, fill a tortilla and enjoy!

Prep Ahead

In a small mixing bowl, add the miso paste, rice vinegar and sesame oil. Mix them well until the miso paste dissolves, then add the water in. Once you get a unified mixture, add the sesame seeds.

Split the miso dressing in half: Half will be used for the tofu marinade and the other half for the wrap.

Place the tofu in a mixing bowl and pour half of the marinade on top. Allow the tofu to marinate for at least 20 minutes, but you may leave it in the fridge overnight as well.

The iceberg lettuce, carrots and cabbage can also be shredded and placed in a Ziploc® bag overnight. Alternatively, you may buy shredded carrots and cabbage so that when you are ready to make the wrap, the veggies are prepared already.

Cooking Method

Use a grill or a nonstick pan to prepare the tofu. Spray some olive oil on the pan, then add the tofu cubes. Sauté them for about 2 minutes, or until the tofu browns on all sides.

Alternatively, you can prepare the tofu in an air fryer by baking it at 400°F (200°C) for about 8 minutes.

Add the shredded iceberg lettuce, carrots and cabbage in a mixing bowl and pour some of the saved marinade on top. Mix the veggies really well with your hands, as the veggies will soften a bit with hand pressure.

Take 1 tortilla and add half of the veggie mixture and half of the tofu. Fold the tortilla in a roll like a burrito or in quarters, making a triangle. Repeat the process with the second tortilla.

Tuna Salad Seaweed Wrap

Yield: 2 servings

Seaweed is often overlooked, but it's a rather nutritious sea vegetable. That's right—it's a veggie, although the dried form we usually see it in does not look like it at all. Seaweed contains a great many vitamins and minerals, plus fiber and omega-3 fats. This antioxidant-rich vegetable is not to be missed when getting creative in the kitchen: Use nori sheets for sushi rolls and wraps, such as the one below, and dried wakame for soups. At most major grocery stores you can even find seaweed snacks, which are seasoned nori sheets that are cut in small rectangles. These snack sheets can be eaten with rice and fresh veggies, making a perfect healthy afternoon snack!

Ingredients

2 (6-oz [170-g]) cans tuna in water, drained

½ cup (55 g) shredded carrot

2 cups (40 g) arugula

1 tbsp (15 ml) olive oil

1 tbsp (15 ml) Dijon mustard

4 dried nori seaweed sheets

Prep Ahead

Add the tuna, carrot and arugula in a mixing bowl. Mix the olive oil and mustard, then pour it over the tuna mixture. You can store this in a container over the next 2 days in the fridge or use it right away.

Cooking Method

Take one nori sheet and add a quarter of the tuna mixture right along the edge. Roll it up like a burrito. In order to close it, just wet the edge of the sheet. Repeat with the other three sheets until you use up all the tuna. Cut each tuna roll in thirds and enjoy!

Meal Prep Notes

For the freshest option for this lunch, I suggest you prepare the tuna mixture ahead of time, but roll the wrap fresh on the day of. It takes only 2 minutes!

Shrimp Fried Rice

Yield: 2–3 servings

This is one of my favorite dishes to make because the macronutrients are balanced really well. I love how the delicate flavor of the shrimp is not overpowered by the vegetables and rice, and the egg is a perfect binder of the three. Fried rice is also one of those dishes where you can get creative with the vegetables you use and is one of the best dishes to make when you need to clean out your fridge. I am sure at some point you've ended up with half a carrot, one celery stick, a small onion and one red pepper? Well, this is your go-to in that case, even if you do not have any additional protein to add—it's great even when just made with veggies. But if you wish to make a plant-based version, I suggest you add some edamame, shiitake or portobello mushrooms to the dish. They all have fiber and protein, which will make this dish filling even without meat or fish.

Ingredients

Shrimp Marinade

¼ tsp gochugaru chili flakes

¼ tsp lemongrass spice

½ tsp fresh grated ginger

1 large clove garlic, grated

1 tbsp (15 ml) olive oil

Fried Rice

½ lb (227 g) shrimp, about 21 shrimp (marinated ahead per Prep Ahead steps)

1 small yellow pepper, finely chopped

1 small green pepper, finely chopped

½ green zucchini, cut in small cubes

1 scallion, green and white part, finely chopped

1 small carrot, minced

1 tbsp (15 ml) olive oil

¾ tsp Himalayan salt

3 cups (558 g) cooked rice (page 14)

2 tbsp (30 ml) soy sauce and 1 tsp sesame oil, mixed and set aside

1 egg

(Continued)

Shrimp Fried Rice (Continued)

Prep Ahead

To prep the shrimp, first prepare the marinade. In a bowl, place the gochugaru, lemongrass, ginger, garlic and olive oil and stir to combine them. Add the shrimp to a glass container with a lid and pour the marinade over them. You can marinate the shrimp for up to 2 days, but ensure you marinate them for at least 30 minutes before you make the dish.

There are two ways to prep the veggies for this dish. One is to prep and store the veggies fresh. Chop or cube the peppers, zucchini, scallion and carrot, place them in a silicone or Ziploc® bag and store them in the fridge.

Another way is to sauté the veggies as per the instructions to the right, cool them down and store them in the fridge. The next day, transfer them to a pan again and heat them up. Proceed with the recipe as if you just sautéed the veggies!

In the instructions written to the right, we are using freshly chopped and cubed veggies.

Cooking Method

Add the olive oil to a pan and once it's warm, add in the peppers, zucchini, scallion, carrot and Himalayan salt. Sauté the veggies for about 4 minutes over medium heat. Add the shrimp along with any liquid from the marinade and continue sautéing until the shrimp turns pale pink, about 4 to 5 minutes.

Add the rice and then the soy sauce and sesame oil mixture and stir until it all incorporates well. After about 2 minutes, make a circle with a wooden spoon in the middle of the pan and drop the egg in.

Stir vigorously until the egg starts cooking. Once you see the egg scramble in the middle of the pan, turn off the heat and give it a good stir so that the egg is well mixed in with the rice and shrimp.

Meal Prep Notes

Enjoy one serving of this dish and allow the rest to cool down. Once it has cooled, place the fried rice in a glass container and store it in the fridge for up to 3 days.

When you are ready to serve it, warm it up on the stove in a nonstick pan or in the microwave or steam oven.

Takeout-Style Kung Pao Chicken

Yield: 4 servings

I love re-creating dishes from restaurants we eat at. Guessing what ingredients are used and how the dish is made is always fun for me to figure out. Sometimes I even ask the waiter if I am not sure, and most of the time they are ready to spill the beans!

This is a really fun way to transform the pretty simple chicken breast into something you want to eat every day. In this recipe we use cornstarch and apple cider vinegar to preserve the juiciness of the chicken as it cooks. Fresh scallions, garlic and ginger add a perfect contrast to a creamy balsamic vinegar and soy sauce glaze.

In this dish we use Korean chili flakes, or gochugaru. These are not as spicy as chili peppers, and they even taste different. Another recipe where you can taste gochugaru is in Bibimbap with Juicy Sirloin, Cucumbers, Shiitake Mushrooms and Carrots (page 88). In that recipe we use gochugaru paste, which is made out of the gochugaru chilis.

Meal Prep Notes

Add one serving of chicken to a plate along with one serving of jasmine or basmati rice (page 14).

Allow the rest of the chicken to cool down, then portion the chicken and rice and store them together in single-portion storage containers. To warm it up, use a nonstick pan or the microwave.

Ingredients

1½ lb (680 g) chicken breast, cubed
3 tbsp (45 ml) olive oil, divided
2 tbsp (16 g) cornstarch
1 tbsp (15 ml) apple cider vinegar
2 tbsp (30 ml) balsamic vinegar glaze
4 tbsp (60 ml) soy sauce
4 tbsp (64 g) tomato paste
1–1½ tsp gochugaru chili flakes
2 tbsp (6 g) chopped scallions
3 cloves garlic, minced
1 small piece fresh ginger, minced
½–1 tsp Himalayan salt
3 tbsp (27 g) unsalted peanuts
Basmati or jasmine rice (page 14)

Prep Ahead

Add the chicken to a bowl and add 1 tablespoon (15 ml) of olive oil, cornstarch and apple cider vinegar. Toss it and let it rest for about 15 minutes or overnight.

To make the chicken glaze, in a mixing bowl, add the balsamic glaze, soy sauce, tomato paste and chili flakes. Stir the glaze until you get a smooth consistency.

Cooking Method

In a medium size pan, add 2 tablespoons (30 ml) of olive oil along with the scallions, garlic and ginger. Sauté them for about 2 minutes, then add the marinated chicken and cook until the chicken becomes white on all sides.

Add the glaze, salt and peanuts. Toss the chicken for another 3 to 4 minutes or until the chicken is cooked through.

*See image on page 80.

Fiesta Time

Welcome to a deliciously fun chapter that is very colorful and filled with much flavor. Spices used in Mexican cuisine are bold and warming, and when combined, they add so much depth to the dishes. From Turkey Chili (page 107), Slow-Cooked Pulled Pork Quesadillas (page 116) and Weeknight Taco Skillet with Grass-Fed Beef (page 123) to Rice and Lentils with Caramelized Onions (page 119), Baked Chipotle-Lime Salmon (page 124) and Baked Shrimp and Beans (page 111), this chapter will bring a true fiesta to your home!

Turkey Chili

Yield: 4 servings

Over the years, I've used ground turkey in this dish in order to make it as lean as I can, but feel free to use ground grass-fed beef or veal. Also, you may use black beans instead of red kidney beans and, if you like more texture, you can use crushed tomatoes instead of tomato puree. The chili powder blend I use for this dish, as well as some other dishes you will find in this chapter, is a mix of Mexican spices such as chili peppers, cumin, garlic, oregano, coriander, cloves and allspice. You can find this blend in most major grocery stores, but if you can't, cumin and plain chili powder do wonders for this delicious dish!

Ingredients

2 tbsp (30 ml) olive oil

1 yellow onion, chopped

2 cloves garlic, minced

1 small green pepper, chopped

1 lb (454 g) ground turkey

1 (15-oz [425-g]) can red kidney beans, drained and rinsed

1½ tsp cumin

½ tsp garlic powder

2 tsp chili powder blend (see note above)

1½ tsp Himalayan salt

3 cups (720 ml) tomato puree or crushed tomatoes

3 cups (720 ml) water or chicken broth

Cooking Method

In a medium size pot, add the olive oil, and when it's warm, add the onion, garlic and pepper. Sauté them for about 2 minutes, then add the ground turkey in. Cook, stirring it often, until the meat is no longer pink, about 5 minutes.

Add the beans in as well as the cumin, garlic powder, chili powder and salt. Stir to combine them, then add the tomato puree and water. Bring the chili to a boil, then cover it with the lid and lower the heat to medium-low. Cook the chili for about 30 minutes. You will know the chili is cooked when some of the liquid has evaporated and the chili has a thick texture.

Meal Prep Notes

Pour one serving into a bowl to enjoy fresh and allow the rest to cool down. Separate the chili into single-portion containers with lids and store it in the fridge over the next 3 to 5 days or freeze it for up to 1 month.

This turkey chili is also wonderful when served with some plain rice (page 14). Just add one serving to a serving of chili and enjoy an even more filling dish! This also serves as a great complete meal prep lunch that you can take to school or work.

One-Pan Mexican Rice
with Chicken

Yield: 4–6 servings

I call this dish "one and done"! It is really nice to be able to make a dish that is a complete meal and fits in one pan.

This rice dish is very aromatic, especially because of the cumin and garlic powder. The mustard-marinated chicken blends in perfectly with these flavors, and the best part is, because we used mustard in the marinade, the chicken will not dry out but rather will stay perfectly juicy!

I love serving this with a large mixed-green salad with some scallions, olive oil and lemon.

Ingredients

2 lb (908 g) chicken (1 double chicken breast + 4 wings + 1 drumstick)

3 tbsp (45 ml) mustard

4 tbsp (60 ml) olive oil, divided

2 tsp Himalayan salt, divided

1 green pepper, grated

½ zucchini, grated

1 onion, grated

½ carrot, grated

½ tsp basil

½ tsp oregano

½ tsp cumin

½ tsp garlic powder

1 tsp red paprika

1 tbsp (16 g) tomato paste

2 cups (400 g) uncooked long grain rice (jasmine or basmati)

3¼ cups (780 ml) water

Fresh parsley for serving

Prep Ahead

Add the chicken to a Ziploc® bag and then add the mustard, 2 tablespoons (30 ml) of olive oil and 1 teaspoon of salt. Marinate it for at least 30 minutes, or overnight.

Grate the pepper, zucchini, onion and carrot and set them aside in a small mixing bowl. If you're not using them right away, you may store the veggies in a Ziploc® bag or a storage container in the fridge overnight.

Cooking Method

Preheat the oven to 425°F (220°C).

Add 2 tablespoons (30 ml) of olive oil to an ovenproof pan and when it's warm, add the pepper, zucchini, onion and carrot. Sauté them for about 1 minute, then add the basil, oregano, cumin, garlic powder, red paprika and 1 teaspoon of salt. Stir until combined, then add the tomato paste, rice and water.

Remove the pan from the heat. With a wooden spoon, make some space for the chicken, then place the chicken in. Distribute the rice evenly, then pop it in the oven, uncovered. If you do not have an ovenproof pan, use any type of stove top pan to make the rice, then transfer it to a baking dish.

Bake the rice and chicken at 425°F (220°C) for about 15 minutes, then lower the heat to 400°F (200°C), cover the pan with foil and bake it for another 40 minutes. You may uncover it for the last 4 to 5 minutes and turn the broiler on the high setting if you want to crisp up the chicken.

Meal Prep Note

This dish can be stored in the fridge for up to 5 days or frozen for up to a month.

Baked Shrimp and Beans

Yield: 4 servings

It would never even have crossed my mind to combine shrimp and beans until I found a recipe similar to this one in an issue of Bon Appétit magazine a few years ago. The combination of the two seemed very strange to me, but the photograph of the dish looked amazing, so I decided to give it a try. The dish ended up being incredible, way beyond my expectations! Fast-forward to last spring, when we were traveling in Spain, and little did we know, you can find shrimp and beans on almost every menu as it's one of Spain's delicacies.

Ever since then, I have been making this recipe my own way, each time a little differently. This version here is one of the ones I make the most. The dish is wonderful when enjoyed fresh but perhaps even better the next day because the flavors marinate even more.

Ingredients

About 1.6 lb (725 g) shrimp

2 tsp minced garlic

1 tsp red paprika

1–1½ tsp Himalayan salt, divided

½ tsp crushed red pepper

3 tbsp (45 ml) olive oil, divided

1 bay leaf

¼ tsp crushed red pepper (optional)

2 whole cloves garlic

4 (14-oz [400-g]) cans white butter beans, drained and rinsed

2 (14-oz [400-g]) cans chopped or crushed tomatoes

12 oz (350 ml) water or seafood stock

1 tbsp (2 g) fresh basil, chopped (optional)

Fresh microgreens (optional)

Black pepper to taste

(Continued)

Baked Shrimp and Beans (Continued)

Prep Ahead

In a Ziploc® bag, add the shrimp, minced garlic, red paprika, 1 teaspoon of salt, crushed red pepper and 1 tablespoon (15 ml) of olive oil. Mix it and let it marinate for at least 30 minutes or overnight. If you choose the latter, ensure the shrimp is at room temperature for about 15 minutes before proceeding with the recipe.

Meal Prep Notes

Any leftover servings of baked shrimp and beans can be placed in a storage container once the dish has cooled down completely. Place it in the fridge and enjoy it over the next 3 days. To warm it up, place it in a pan with a few table-spoons of water and cover it with a lid.

If you wish, you can cook the beans with the tomato sauce ahead of time. Once you cook the beans on the stove top, allow them to cool, then add them to a storage container and place it in the fridge. The next day, heat up the beans on the stove, add the shrimp and pop them in the oven. Proceed with baking as instructed.

Cooking Method

Preheat the oven to 425°F (220°C).

Add 2 tablespoons (30 ml) of olive oil to a large ovenproof pan and when it's warm, add the bay leaf, crushed red pepper and garlic cloves. Sauté them for just a few seconds and then add the beans, tomatoes and water. If you use seafood stock, you may not need to add salt. If you use water, add about ½ teaspoon of Himalayan salt.

Bring it to a boil, then lower the heat to medium and cook it for about 15 minutes, or until about a third of the liquid evaporates. Once the sauce thickens, it's time to add the shrimp.

Add the shrimp on top of the beans, distributing them evenly, and then just gently dip them inside the sauce with a fork or a spoon. Place the pan in the oven and bake the shrimp and beans for about 15 to 17 minutes. You may use the broiler on the high setting for the last 3 to 4 minutes if you want to get a nice crisp on top.

Carefully take the pan out of the oven, remembering that the handle is hot. It is best to place an oven mitt on the handle and leave it on once you take the pan out of the oven. Allow the beans to cool down for about 15 minutes before digging in. The dish gets really hot and it cools down slowly, kind of like a hot soup, so just be extra careful when handling it.

You may garnish the shrimp and beans with fresh basil or microgreens, add black pepper to taste and even add a little drizzle of good-quality olive oil.

I love to serve this dish with some plain rice (page 14), but it is also wonderful when served on its own.

Grilled Chicken Fajitas

with Peppers and Onions

Yield: 4–6 servings

This is a dish that I would highly recommend for your next BBQ party! The chicken can be prepared ahead and so can the vegetables. All you need to do when the guests arrive is to quickly grill or panfry it all. Add some jasmine rice, lettuce wraps or tortillas, and the party is on its way!

If you need more dishes to add to the party, try Grilled Shrimp Tacos with Homemade Salsa (page 120) and Slow-Cooked Pulled Pork Quesadillas (page 116) as well as Turkey Chili (page 107). And for the starter nibbles while you are preparing dinner, serve some grain-free tortilla chips, salsa and guacamole. Talk about a real fiesta!

Ingredients

Fajitas

1½ lb (680 g) chicken breast, cut into strips

1 tsp chili powder blend

1 lime, squeezed

2 tsp cumin, divided

1½–1¾ tsp Himalayan salt, divided

3 tbsp (45 ml) olive oil, divided, plus more for basting the pan

5 peppers (red, yellow, green), cut into strips

1 medium purple onion, thinly sliced

For Serving

Fresh butter lettuce or iceberg lettuce

Jasmine or basmati rice (page 14)

Homemade Salsa (page 120; optional, but a delicious add-on!)

(Continued)

Grilled Chicken Fajitas (Continued)

Prep Ahead

In a large Ziploc® bag, place the chicken breast strips along with the chili powder, lime juice, 1 teaspoon of cumin, 1 teaspoon of salt and 2 tablespoons (30 ml) of olive oil. Close the bag and mix everything well until the chicken strips are evenly coated. Let the chicken marinate overnight or for at least 30 minutes.

Cutting the peppers in strips can be time consuming, so this is something you can do ahead of time as well. Simply cut the peppers and place them in a storage container, and store them in the fridge until you're ready to use them.

Cooking Method

Prepare a cast-iron pan or grill pan for grilling the chicken by basting it with olive oil and warming it up.

Meanwhile, add 1 tablespoon (15 ml) of olive oil to a saucepan and when it's warm, add the peppers and onion. Add 1 teaspoon of cumin and ½ to ¾ teaspoon of salt, stir to combine them and continue sautéing the peppers for about 3 to 4 minutes. When the peppers are tender and the onion is translucent, remove them from the heat and set them aside on a plate.

Add the chicken strips to the pan and grill them for about 4 to 5 minutes. The chicken will cook fast as it's cut into strips.

Alternatively, you may air fry the chicken at 400°F (200°C) for about 6 to 8 minutes. To serve the fajitas fresh, place about four large lettuce leaves on each plate, then add some rice, peppers and chicken in each.

Meal Prep Notes

How big the lettuce leaves are will determine how much you can add to them. But adding about 1 tablespoon (16 g) of rice, 2 tablespoons (16 g) of chicken and 1 tablespoon (7 g) of peppers per lettuce leaf will be sufficient. If you're adding salsa, pour a teaspoon right on top of the already juicy chicken.

To store the fajitas, cool down the peppers and chicken as well as the rice if you made extra. In each glass container, add one serving of chicken, peppers and rice. Store them in the fridge over the next 3 days.

To warm up a serving, add it to a saucepan, stir to combine it and cook until it's warm enough to your taste. Alternatively, you may warm it up in a glass container in the microwave or steam oven.

Another idea for serving this dish the next day would be with some whole grain or almond flour tortillas instead of rice. Just warm up a tortilla, add some chicken and some peppers, wrap it up and enjoy!

Slow-Cooked Pulled Pork Quesadillas

Yield: 6 servings

Quesadillas are incredibly versatile and can be customized to suit different tastes and dietary preferences. They can be made with gluten-free tortillas, almond flour tortillas or white or whole wheat tortillas, vegan cheese or regular cheese, and animal-based protein or vegan protein such as beans. As a filling, you can truly use a wide range of ingredients to cater to individual preferences and dietary restrictions.

Quesadillas are often served with a variety of accompaniments such as salsa, guacamole, sour cream or pico de gallo, adding extra flavors and textures to the dish. One of the healthy swaps I use is serving Greek yogurt instead of sour cream. Greek yogurt can be just as creamy as sour cream, but it's lower in fat and calories. I typically opt for at least 2% fat, as the ones that are fat-free tend not to be as creamy.

Quesadillas got their name from "queso," which means cheese, but while cheese is a staple ingredient in quesadillas, I still go heavy on the main protein, and in this case that is juicy pulled pork.

Ingredients

1 cup (240 ml) tomato puree

¼ cup (60 ml) Worcester sauce

1 tbsp (12 g) Himalayan salt

1 tbsp (8 g) garlic powder

1 tbsp (6 g) cumin

2 tbsp (30 ml) olive oil

23 oz (650 g) pork tenderloin, cut in half

1 large onion, sliced

¼–½ cup (60–120 ml) water

6 medium tortillas (whole wheat, almond flour, corn)

6 tbsp (42 g) shredded part-skim mozzarella cheese or vegan cheese, divided

2 cups (134 g) shredded iceberg lettuce

Prep Ahead

To prepare the marinade, add tomato puree, Worcester sauce, salt, garlic powder, cumin and olive oil to a mixing bowl. Stir to combine them.

Place the pork tenderloin in a slow cooker, or in a cast-iron pot if you are using the oven for baking. Pour the sauce over the pork tenderloin and mix it well until the pork is coated nicely. Layer the onion on top of the pork, then pour ¼ cup (59 ml) water on the bottom of the slow cooker (or ½ cup [118 ml] if you are using a cast-iron pot).

If you are using a slow cooker, turn it on and cook for 6 hours on low. When it's done, shred the pork with a fork and let it marinate in the juices for about 10 minutes or so.

Should you decide to use the oven, preheat the oven to 425°F (220°C). When you add the pork in, cover it with a lid or foil, lower the heat to 375°F (190°C) and bake the pork for at least 3 hours. Check the pork halfway through to ensure there is enough liquid on the bottom of the pot, and baste the pork tenderloin with some liquid from the bottom of the pan. Once it's cooked, separate the meat with a fork and let it rest in the juices for a few minutes.

If you're using the meat right away, proceed with the cooking instructions at right. If you are preparing the meat for the next day, allow the meat to cool down and then add it to a storage container. You can store the meat in the fridge overnight or for up to 5 days. When you're ready to serve it, just place it in a pan with some liquid and warm it up on the stove top.

Cooking Method

In a grill pan, add 1 tortilla. Grill it on one side and as soon as it's warm, sprinkle 1 tablespoon (7 g) of shredded cheese all over the tortilla.

When the cheese starts melting, add a few tablespoons of meat (about 8 oz or 220 g) and some iceberg lettuce (about a third of what you prepared).

Add another tablespoon (7 g) of shredded mozzarella over the meat and then top it off with a second tortilla. Slowly flip the quesadilla onto the other side and grill it for just a few seconds. Transfer it onto a plate, cut it into eighths and enjoy!

You may decide to make single-serve quesadillas. To do that, add 1 tortilla in the pan, sprinkle cheese on one half, then add the meat and iceberg lettuce. Flip the tortilla over and fold it in half. Grill it for about 1 minute, then slowly flip it over to the other side. Your single-serve quesadilla will be ready as soon as the cheese melts, about 1 minute.

Meal Prep Notes

If you wish to save the leftovers, allow the quesadillas to cool down to room temperature and then place them in glass containers and store them in the fridge. Ready-made quesadillas will be best if eaten cold, as warming them up in the pan may dry them out and the microwave will make them soggy. But you definitely won't be disappointed if you try them cold!

As mentioned in the notes in the Prep Ahead section, pulled pork may be stored in the fridge for up to 5 days. And believe it or not, the taste stays the same!

Rice and Lentils
with Caramelized Onions

Yield: 4 servings

When I first moved to the USA over 20 years ago, rice was not something that I liked eating. One of my best friends at the time was a really good cook and she invited me over for dinner one night. When she asked me if I liked lentils and rice, I had a long stare at her, as I had never even heard of lentils. Little did I know that the dish was going to become one of my very favorites.

When paired together, rice and lentils are truly wonderful, and the caramelized onions and cumin add the perfect balance of flavors.

I suggest you try this as a side dish with Baked Chipotle-Lime Salmon (page 124) or any of your favorite proteins, such as simple grilled chicken or pan-seared tofu.

Ingredients

1½ cups (360 ml) water

1½ tsp cumin, divided

1 cup (200 g) uncooked white rice (jasmine or basmati)

3 tbsp (45 ml) olive oil

4 large onions, sliced thinly

1 tsp salt

2 cups (396 g) cooked lentils (page 15)

Cooking Method

To make the rice, add the water and ½ teaspoon of cumin to a medium size saucepan and bring it to a boil. Add the rice, cover it and lower the heat to low. Cook, covered, for about 18 to 20 minutes.

Meanwhile, add the olive oil to a large pan and when it's warm, add the sliced onions in. Sauté them for a few minutes until the onions become translucent and then add 1 teaspoon of cumin and salt. Continue sautéing until the onion caramelizes. Remove the onion from the heat and set it aside.

In a serving bowl, add the lentils and rice and toss to combine them. Add the caramelized onion on top and serve it warm.

Meal Prep Notes

Any leftovers may be stored in an airtight container and refrigerated for about 3 to 4 days. This dish also freezes well for up to 1 month.

To warm it up, you can use a steam oven or microwave.

You may prepare the rice and lentils ahead of time, combine them and place them in a storage container. The next day, follow the directions for preparing caramelized onions and enjoy them fresh.

Grilled Shrimp Tacos
with Homemade Salsa

Yield: 4 servings

This is probably one of my favorite things to eat during the summer. In this combination of flavors, the refreshing shrimp and lime meet Mexican spices to bring you a delicious savory-yet-sweet dish. Homemade salsa and shredded purple cabbage add the perfect crisp to every bite. If you wish to make this dish low carb, you can use iceberg lettuce leaves instead of tortillas. And trust me when I tell you, you may love this dish even more!

Ingredients

Garlic Chili Shrimp

2 lb (907 g) raw shrimp (about 40)
1 lime, squeezed
1 tsp garlic powder
½ tsp cumin
½ tsp chili powder blend
½ tsp Himalayan salt

Homemade Salsa

1 cup (180 g) finely chopped tomatoes
⅓ cup (53 g) finely chopped red onion
¼ cup (15 g) fresh parsley, minced
1 lime, squeezed
½ tsp Himalayan salt

Tacos

Olive oil spray
8 small whole grain or almond flour tortillas
1 avocado, mashed
2 cups (140 g) shredded purple cabbage
Sriracha or hot sauce (optional)

Prep Ahead

In a Ziploc® bag, add the shrimp along with the lime juice, garlic powder, cumin, chili powder and salt and place it in the fridge overnight. If you do not have time to leave it in the fridge overnight, you can marinate it for about 30 minutes. This will be sufficient time for the shrimp to develop nicely in flavor.

To prepare the salsa ahead of time, add the tomatoes, onion and parsley to a glass jar. Add the lime juice and salt, mix them well, then cover the jar and place it in the fridge. Salsa prepared like this can stay fresh for up to 3 days.

Cooking Method

Spray a nonstick or a cast-iron pan with olive oil. When it's warm, add the shrimp and panfry them for about 3 minutes. Flip them to the other side and fry them for another 3 minutes or until the shrimp is pink and tender.

Remove the shrimp from the heat and set them aside. You can also use the grill to prepare the shrimp the same way you would prepare them on the stove top.

To serve this dish, take 2 small tortillas per person and on each, add 1 tablespoon (14 g) of mashed avocado, 5 to 6 shrimp, 1 tablespoon (15 ml) of homemade salsa and 2 tablespoons (12 g) of shredded cabbage. For a perfect finishing touch, add sriracha or hot sauce!

Weeknight Taco Skillet
with Grass-Fed Beef

Yield: 2 servings

Whether you decide to meal prep this dish or make it the night of, it will come together so quickly. The beauty of quick, delicious and nutritious meals is that you will spend less time in the kitchen and more time actually enjoying the meal. In our busy lives, it is so important to slow down and sit down during meal times to truly realize what's on the plate.

The combination of rice and beans is always winning, and when you add steak to it as well, this meal becomes a true protein powerhouse! If you decide to make this dish when you're having some friends over, combine it with Slow-Cooked Pulled Pork Quesadillas (page 116), which you can make as an appetizer. Your guests will be well-fed and pleased!

Ingredients

¾ lb (340 g) sirloin or rib eye steak

1 tbsp (15 ml) olive oil, plus more for greasing the pan

1 tbsp (15 ml) Worcester sauce

1 cup (240 ml) tomato puree

1 (15-oz [425-g]) can black beans, drained and rinsed

1 tsp cumin

½ tsp Himalayan salt

1 cup (186 g) cooked rice (page 14)

1 tbsp (4 g) fresh parsley or cilantro

½ avocado, cubed

Prep Ahead

Add the steak to a Ziploc® bag along with the olive oil and Worcester sauce. Rub it well, close the bag and let the steak marinate overnight or for at least 20 minutes before preparing it. If you leave it overnight in the fridge, ensure that you take it out and leave it at room temperature for at least 10 minutes before cooking it.

Cooking Method

Heat up a cast-iron skillet, then grease it with some olive oil. Add the steak and pan sear it on one side for about 4 minutes, then flip it to the other side and cook it for another 2 minutes. Depending on how thick the steak is, this will give you a medium cooked steak.

Take the steak out of the pan and leave it on the cutting board to rest while you prepare the rest of the dish.

Scrape up any meat bits and pieces from the pan, and grease it again. Heat it up, then add the tomato puree, beans, cumin and salt. Bring the sauce to a boil, then lower the heat and cook it for just 2 more minutes. Remove it from the heat.

Slice the steak and add it to the pan along with the cooked rice. Add the fresh parsley or cilantro and some fresh avocado. Enjoy it warm!

Meal Prep Notes

If you have any leftovers of this dish, once you cool it down to room temperature, store it in a glass container with a lid in the fridge overnight. This dish is best when warmed up on the stove in the cast-iron skillet or in the microwave.

Baked Chipotle-Lime Salmon

Yield: 2 servings

Salmon is known for its natural oils, omega-3s, which contribute to its distinctive taste and moistness—so we do not need to use oil when preparing it. Whether grilled, baked or pan seared, the delectable flavors of salmon are further enhanced by its ability to absorb and complement a variety of seasonings, making it a favorite choice for countless savory recipes.

The homemade chipotle spice rub can be used with other types of fish as well. I've tried it with halibut and mahi mahi and it was delicious. Beyond fish, this rub can also be used on turkey or chicken.

Beyond the baked salmon recipe below, here are four more different ways you can prepare salmon:

Teriyaki Style: Mix 1 tbsp (15 ml) soy sauce, 1 tsp honey, ¼ tsp garlic powder and ¼ tsp ground ginger. It's best to bake it in the oven if dressed this way.

Dijon Mustard: Mix 1 tbsp (15 ml) Dijon mustard and 1 tsp fresh dill. Bake it in the oven, panfry it or grill it.

Sesame: Spray the salmon with some olive oil, then sprinkle sesame seeds on top. Bake it as usual, or you can also panfry it or grill it.

Steamed: Place the salmon in parchment paper. Layer some freshly cut bell pepper on top of the salmon and sprinkle salt on top, then wrap the parchment paper around it, pulling all four corners of the parchment toward the center and twisting them together to close. Place it in the oven and bake it as usual.

Ingredients

2 (6-oz [170-g]) pieces of salmon

2 tsp ponzu sauce

1 tbsp (7 g) red paprika (you can use smoked)

1 tbsp (6 g) chili powder blend

1 tsp garlic powder

1 tsp cumin

½ tsp oregano

½ tsp coriander

½ tsp Himalayan salt

1 whole lime (rind grated, save the lime juice for salmon)

Prep Ahead

Place the salmon in a container with a lid, add the ponzu sauce, rub it in, cover the salmon and store it in the fridge overnight or for at least 20 minutes.

The chipotle-lime rub can be prepared any time you see fit. Since it's a dry spice, it can last a very long time in your pantry. In a mixing bowl, simply add the paprika, chili powder blend, garlic powder, cumin, oregano, coriander, salt, and lime zest. Mix the spice and place it in a small jar.

Cooking Method

Preheat the oven to 425°F (220°C). Place the salmon on a baking tray and bake it for about 15 minutes. You may turn on the broiler on the high setting at the end to crisp up the top a little bit more.

When you take the salmon out, squeeze some lime juice on each of the slices and sprinkle some of the chipotle-lime seasoning on top .

California Bowls

For some reason, certain dishes just taste so much better when they are served in a bowl. This is especially true with leftovers! Two-day-old roasted veggies can easily become a new dish just by combining them with some freshly made brown rice and a good dressing.

In this chapter you will find a selection of recipes that are plant based. Among my favorites are the Roasted Sweet Potato Kale Bowl with Avocado Garlic Dressing (page 140) and the Fall Harvest Bowl with Roasted Butternut Squash, Apples and Walnuts (page 143). For seafood lovers, the Shrimp and Orange Lover Bowl (page 136) is wonderful as well as the Grilled Ahi Tuna Bowl with Edamame, Spiralized Carrots and Cucumbers (page 131). And if you are a fan of one-pan meals, be sure to try the One and Done Roasted Brussels Sprouts and Chicken Bowl (page 135).

Teriyaki Mushrooms

with Purple Cabbage and Brown Rice Bowl

Yield: 2 servings

I don't know if you have ever tried roasted cabbage, but it is absolutely delicious. I often bake it in the oven with just some olive oil and Himalayan salt. In fact, if you ever have leftover roasted cabbage, feel free to use it in this dish instead of preparing it as described in the recipe steps.

In this recipe you will find a homemade teriyaki sauce made with soy sauce, maple syrup and spices that is a much healthier version than the store-bought kind.

For additional protein you may add Baked Chipotle-Lime Salmon (page 124) or another style of salmon, Miso-Glazed Tofu (page 97) or simple baked chicken breast using one of the meat marinades from the Protein section (page 16).

Ingredients

Ginger Garlic Mushrooms

1 tbsp (15 ml) sesame oil

1 tbsp (15 ml) soy sauce or coconut aminos

1 tsp maple syrup or honey

½ tsp garlic powder

½ tsp ground ginger

2½ cups (200 g) sliced shiitake mushrooms

Olive oil spray

Teriyaki Sauce

1 tbsp (15 ml) sesame oil

1 tbsp (15 ml) maple syrup or honey

1 tbsp (15 ml) rice vinegar

1 tbsp (15 ml) soy sauce

1 tsp sesame seeds

Bowl Base

1 tsp sesame oil

1 tsp olive oil

2 shallots, sliced

2 cups (140 g) purple cabbage, shredded

2 cups (372 g) cooked brown rice (page 14)

(Continued)

Teriyaki Mushrooms (Continued)

Prep Ahead

In a small bowl, prepare the mushroom marinade by adding the sesame oil, soy sauce, maple syrup, garlic powder and ginger. Stir it and set it aside.

Add the mushrooms to another mixing bowl and pour the marinade you prepared on top. Toss them and let them marinate for at least 20 minutes or overnight.

To prepare the teriyaki sauce, in a small mixing bowl, add the sesame oil, maple syrup, rice vinegar, soy sauce and sesame seeds. Mix it, cover it and save the sauce until you're ready to use it. You do not have to refrigerate it.

Cooking Method

Add the sesame and olive oil to a nonstick or cast-iron pan and after it warms up, add the shallots as well as the purple cabbage. Toss and panfry until the cabbage softens, about 5 minutes. The cabbage will be nicely roasted, as if you baked it in the oven.

Transfer the cabbage to a serving bowl where you have already plated the rice.

In the same pan, spray some olive oil, then add the mushrooms and panfry them for about 5 minutes.

Add the mushrooms on top of the cabbage and rice. Pour the prepared teriyaki sauce on top and toss everything to mix it.

Meal Prep Notes

Once you prepare the dish, divide it into two portions. Enjoy one right away and allow the other to cool down, then add it to a storage container with a lid and place it in the fridge. The next day, you may warm it up in the pan on the stove, in the microwave or in a steam oven.

Grilled Ahi Tuna Bowl

with Edamame, Spiralized Carrots and Cucumbers

Yield: 1 serving

Rich in protein but low in fat and easy to prepare, tuna makes a great protein add-on to any grain or vegetable bowl. Tuna is best when made fresh, but storing it for 1 day in the fridge is quite all right as well. Should you need to store tuna for more than 1 day, marinate it, and then you can keep it in the fridge for up to 3 days.

Spiralized veggies make this bowl really fun, but you can certainly skip that step and just thinly slice them. Iceberg lettuce and Boston lettuce are both really great replacements for the arugula.

Ingredients

Tuna

1 tbsp (15 ml) soy or ponzu sauce
1 tsp toasted sesame oil
1 clove garlic, crushed
1 tsp ginger, grated finely
6 oz (170 g) tuna steak
Olive oil spray
2 tbsp (18 g) sesame seeds

Sesame Dressing

2 tbsp (30 ml) olive or avocado oil
1 tbsp (15 ml) rice vinegar
¼ tsp brown sugar
½ tsp Himalayan salt
1 tsp sesame seeds
1 tbsp (3 g) minced scallion

Bowl Base

½ English cucumber, spiralized or sliced thin
1 large carrot, spiralized or sliced thin
2 cups (40 g) arugula
½ cup (85 g) edamame, boiled
¼ avocado, sliced

(Continued)

Grilled Ahi Tuna Bowl (Continued)

Prep Ahead

To prepare the tuna steak, in a small bowl, add the soy sauce, sesame oil, garlic and ginger. Mix it well and then pour it over the tuna. Rub the marinade all over the tuna so it's nicely coated on both sides. Place the tuna in a Ziploc® or silicone bag and let it marinate for at least 30 minutes or overnight in the fridge.

In a small glass jar, add the olive oil, rice vinegar, brown sugar, salt, sesame seeds and scallion. Mix the dressing and set it aside.

Unless you buy spiralized cucumber and carrot, it is much easier to prep these ahead than to spiralize them on the day of. Once you spiralize the carrot, place it in a small container or a jar with a lid and add water to cover the carrot. Store the carrot in the fridge until ready to use. Spiralized cucumber can be placed on a paper towel, wrapped and stored in a large Ziploc® or silicone bag. Place it in the fridge until you're ready to use it.

Cooking Method

Heat up a nonstick or cast-iron pan.

Spray some olive oil spray all over the tuna, then dip the sides into the sesame seeds. Place the tuna on the hot pan and sear it for about 3 minutes on one side, then flip it to the other side. Sear it for another 2 minutes and remove it from the heat. Let the tuna rest for about 5 minutes before slicing it.

If you stored the carrots in water overnight, drain the water, wrap the carrots in a paper towel and pat them dry.

Add the arugula to a large salad bowl along with the spiralized carrots and cucumbers, edamame and avocado. Add the sliced tuna steak and pour some dressing on top. Enjoy it fresh.

> ### Meal Prep Notes
>
> If you wish to save some of this bowl for the next day, you may place it all together in a container with a lid but omit the avocado and the dressing. The dressing should be stored separately and poured over the salad when you wish to eat it.

One and Done Roasted Brussels Sprouts and Chicken Bowl

Yield: 1–2 servings

There is nothing easier than placing all the ingredients in one pan and being done with dinner. Wouldn't you agree? This sheet pan dinner uses just two main ingredients, but you can add more vegetables if you like as well as some freshly cooked rice or quinoa (pages 13–14). Some other veggies that would work really well in this dish are broccoli, cauliflower and cabbage.

I also love this dish as a school or work lunch because it tastes really good even at room temperature or cold. If you would like to make a big batch of this dish, just quadruple the ingredients and make one whole sheet pan of Brussels sprouts and then one of chicken. Once they cool, you can place them in individual storage containers in the fridge. Enjoy them as if they were fresh over the next 3 days!

Ingredients

1 lb (454 g) Brussels sprouts, cleaned and cut in half

2 tbsp (30 ml) olive oil

¾ tsp Himalayan salt, divided

½ lb (227 g) chicken breast

Olive oil spray

¼ tsp red paprika

¼ tsp garlic powder

1 tbsp (15 ml) maple syrup

Cooking Method

Preheat the oven to 400°F (200°C). Line a sheet pan with parchment paper and set it aside.

Add the Brussels sprouts to the sheet pan, then the olive oil and ½ teaspoon of salt. Toss them and distribute them on one side of the pan. Add the chicken breast, then spray it with olive oil and add ¼ teaspoon of salt, red paprika and garlic powder.

Place the pan in the oven and bake everything for about 30 minutes. Once you take the pan out of the oven, let it cool for about 5 minutes.

Cut the chicken breast in strips, then add them to a bowl along with some Brussels sprouts. Pour some maple syrup on top of the Brussels sprouts and enjoy the meal warm.

Meal Prep Notes

To make this meal ahead, follow the directions above. Once the chicken and Brussels sprouts are baked, allow them to cool down completely, then place them in a glass storage container with a lid and place it in the fridge. The next day you can eat this meal cold, or you can warm it up by placing it in an egg pan, adding a couple of tablespoons of water and covering it with a lid. Alternatively, you can use the microwave or steam oven. Maple syrup should be added once the dish is heated up.

Shrimp and Orange Lover Bowl

Yield: 2 servings

Citrusy and light yet very nutrient dense and filling, this shrimp bowl will become your favorite in no time. In this recipe it's really easy to swap the protein, and you can even make it plant based if you use simple pan-seared tofu (make sure you try one of the delicious tofu marinades from the Protein section on page 16).

The dressing can be made in large batches and stored in a glass jar in the fridge for up to 3 days. It tastes really good with any kind of salad, and I love it with baby kale and baby spinach too!

Ingredients

Shrimp Marinade

1 lb (454 g) shrimp (about 16–20)
2 cloves garlic, crushed
½ tsp red paprika
1 tbsp (15 ml) olive oil
Olive oil spray

Apple Cider Orange Dressing

1 large orange, squeezed
2 tbsp (30 ml) olive oil
2 tbsp (30 ml) apple cider vinegar
1 tsp honey
1 small shallot or red onion, sliced

Bowl Base

5 oz (140 g) spring lettuce mix
10 cherry tomatoes
½ large English cucumber, cubed
4 small radishes, sliced
1 small orange, cubed
2 tbsp (22 g) olives, chopped

Prep Ahead

To marinate the shrimp, in a mixing bowl, add the shrimp, garlic, red paprika and olive oil. Toss the shrimp, then cover the bowl and let it marinate for at least 30 minutes or overnight in the fridge.

To prepare the dressing, in a mixing bowl, add the orange juice, olive oil, apple cider vinegar and honey. Whisk the dressing, add the shallot in and stir it to combine.

If you are not using the dressing right away, transfer it to a jar with a lid and store it in the fridge.

Cooking Method

If you kept the shrimp in the fridge overnight, leave them out for about 5 minutes before starting to cook them.

Spray a nonstick grill pan with some olive oil and when the pan is hot, add the shrimp. Grill them for about 3 minutes on one side and 3 on the other.

In a large mixing bowl, add the lettuce, tomatoes, cucumber, radishes, orange cubes and olives. Toss to combine them. Add the shrimp in and pour some dressing over the salad. Toss to combine and enjoy.

Meal Prep Note

If you are not serving both portions of the salad, split the salad base in half, as well as the shrimp and dressing. Transfer the salad base to one bowl, the shrimp to another and the dressing in a third. The next day, combine it all.

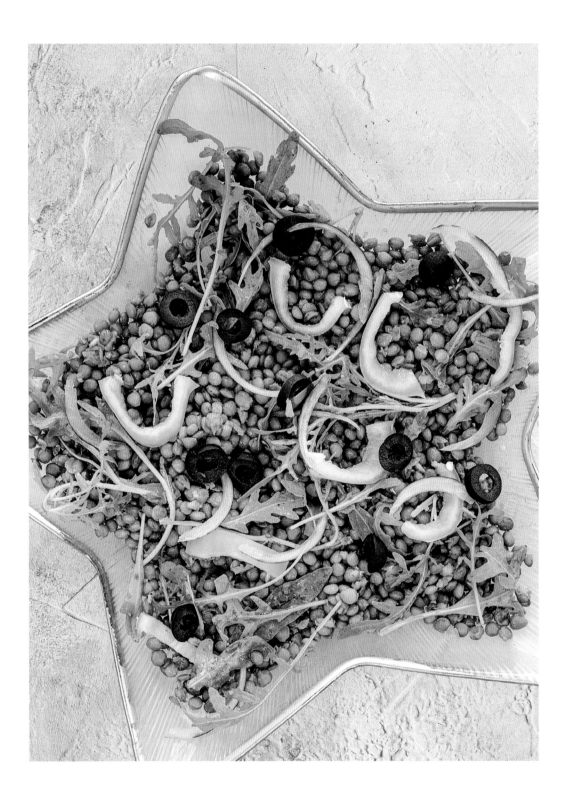

Mediterranean Green Lentil Salad Bowl

Yield: 2–4 servings

Lentils are such a wonderful plant-based source of protein and a true superfood when it comes to fiber content. Unlike beans, lentils do not need to be soaked before cooking as they cook rather fast. Just like with rice and all the grains, it's important to rinse the lentils really well. For easier digestibility you can add a bay leaf during the boiling process.

Ingredients

¾ cup (144 g) dry green lentils, rinsed (or about 2 cups [396 g] cooked lentils [page 15])

3 cups (720 ml) water

½ red onion, sliced thin

1 cup (20 g) arugula, chopped

1 green pepper, sliced

½ cup (90 g) kalamata olives, sliced

2 tbsp (30 ml) olive oil

2 tbsp (30 ml) red or white wine vinegar

½ tsp Himalayan salt

Prep Ahead

In a medium size saucepan, add the lentils and water. Cover and cook them over low heat until the lentils are tender, about 25 minutes. Drain the lentils and allow them to cool down completely.

If you're using the lentils right away, add them to a mixing bowl and proceed with the recipe. And if you're using them the next day, transfer the lentils to a storage container with a lid and store them in the fridge overnight.

Cooking Method

Add the red onion, arugula, pepper and olives to the bowl where you already placed the cooked lentils. Add the olive oil, wine vinegar and salt. Lightly toss to combine everything.

As the arugula may get soggy once you add the dressing in, if you are not planning on having the salad right away, simply store the lentils, vegetables and dressing separately. When you wish to have the salad, all you need to do is combine all the ingredients and toss!

Meal Prep Notes

You can eat this salad as a standalone dish, or you may serve it with some additional protein. Some protein add-ons would be Pan-Seared Whitefish Filets (page 40), Baked Turkey Meatballs (page 65) or Baked Chipotle-Lime Salmon (page 124).

Roasted Sweet Potato Kale Bowl

with Avocado Garlic Dressing

Yield: 2 servings

When you need that extra fiber in your life, turn to this fabulous bowl. Delicious and hearty kale, perfectly roasted sweet potatoes and beans are dressed with creamy avocado dressing with hints of garlic. Sounds complicated, but this bowl is really easy to make and it doesn't take long, especially if you roast some sweet potatoes ahead of time, as described in the Prep Ahead section.

Ingredients

Sweet Potato

1 large sweet potato, cut into large sticks

Olive oil spray

Avocado Garlic Dressing

2 tbsp (30 ml) olive oil

¼ cup (60 ml) water

¼ ripe avocado

2 cloves garlic

1 tbsp (4 g) fresh parsley

½ tsp Himalayan salt

Bowl Base

1 small head of kale (about 10 oz [284 g]), chopped

1 cup (172 g) black beans, rinsed and drained

2 tbsp (20 g) hemp seeds

Prep Ahead

Preheat the oven to 425°F (220°C).

Line a small baking tray with parchment paper, then add the chopped sticks of sweet potato. Spray them with some olive oil and bake them for about 25 to 30 minutes.

Alternatively, you may bake them in an air fryer at 400°F (200°C) for about 18 minutes.

Allow the sweet potato to cool to room temperature. If you're not using it right away, place the sweet potato in a storage container and in the fridge overnight or for up to 5 days.

Cooking Method

To prepare the dressing, in a blender, add the olive oil, water, avocado, garlic, fresh parsley and salt. Blend until the dressing is smooth.

Add the chopped kale to a large mixing bowl and add half the dressing. Mix the salad well by using your hands. Squeezing the kale really helps with softening it up. Add the beans and sweet potatoes and pour the rest of the dressing on top. Sprinkle on some hemp seeds and enjoy!

Meal Prep Notes

If you wish to save one serving of this bowl for the next day, add the kale, beans and sweet potatoes in one storage container and save the dressing separately. The day of, just mix and enjoy!

Fall Harvest Bowl

with Roasted Butternut Squash, Apples and Walnuts

Yield: 2 servings

Nothing says "fall" more than butternut squash, apples and walnuts. This is probably one of the first dishes I make when the roasting season starts. The smell of baked butternut squash is just so incredible and so is the smell of the baked apples. In this recipe we are using fresh apples, but you can certainly use baked ones as well.

As butternut squash is hard to peel and cut, I suggest you buy the precut, prewashed kind that comes already cubed. This will save you at least 10 minutes in preparing this recipe!

The honey mustard dressing can be used in many recipes, not only this one. Next time you make a grilled chicken salad, for example, I suggest you try it with this dressing. Really delicious!

Ingredients

Roasted Squash

1 cup (116 g) cubed fresh butternut squash or pumpkin

Olive oil spray

Honey Mustard Dressing

2 tbsp (30 ml) olive oil

1 tsp yellow mustard

1 tsp whole grain mustard

1 tsp honey

2–3 tbsp (30–45 ml) water

Bowl Base

4 cups (80 g) arugula

2 tbsp (14 g) walnuts, roasted

½ apple, thinly sliced

Prep Ahead

Preheat the oven to 425°F (220°C).

Line a sheet pan with parchment paper, then add the cubed butternut squash. Spray it with olive oil, mix it well and cover it with foil or parchment paper. Place the squash in the oven and bake it for about 30 minutes, or until it is soft. You may uncover the squash for the last 10 minutes so you get a nice browning.

Allow the butternut squash to cool to room temperature and, if you're using it right away, proceed with the recipe. If you're storing it for another day, transfer the butternut squash to a storage container and place it in the fridge for up to 3 to 4 days.

To prepare the dressing, add the olive oil, mustards and honey to a small mixing bowl. Whisk it until it's all well incorporated. Add the water to thin out the dressing. If you like the dressing really runny, you may add more. To store the dressing, add it to a jar with a lid, or you may use it right away.

Cooking Method

In a large mixing bowl, add the arugula, walnuts, sliced apple and butternut squash. Pour some dressing on top and enjoy!

> ### Meal Prep Notes
>
> If you wish to save one serving for the next day, place the salad in one storage container and the dressing in another. Store them in the fridge overnight. When you are ready to enjoy the salad, just toss the ingredients together and enjoy!

Quinoa Galore Bowl

with Mediterranean Dressing

Yield: 4 servings as a side dish, 2 servings as a main

This fiber- and protein-rich quinoa bowl can be modified in so many different ways so that lunch is never boring again. I typically add a roasted veggie and then whatever else I have on hand from the fresh veggie selection. I also love adding microgreens to this bowl, as well as baby kale or arugula. Adding some greens definitely adds another wonderful layer of nutrients as well as flavors. If you prefer brown rice over quinoa, you can swap that in as well! But certainly start with this version and then play around with what you have on hand and what is in season.

Ingredients

Roasted Cauliflower

1 small head cauliflower, cut into small florets (about 2 cups [650 g] when roasted)

Olive oil spray

Mediterranean Dressing

¼ cup (60 ml) olive oil

⅛ cup (30 ml) white wine vinegar

½ lemon, squeezed

1 tsp basil

1 tsp oregano

1 tsp Himalayan salt

Bowl Base

2 cups (370 g) cooked quinoa (page 13)

1 cup (130 g) Persian cucumber, chopped

1 cup (150 g) cherry tomatoes, cut in half

2 scallions, chopped

1 celery rib, chopped

Prep Ahead

Preheat the oven to 425°F (220°C).

Line a small baking sheet with parchment paper, then add the cauliflower florets. Spray them with olive oil and place them in the oven. Bake the cauliflower for about 25 minutes.

Alternatively, you may use an air fryer and bake them at 400°F (200°C) for about 12 minutes.

Allow the cauliflower to cool to room temperature. If you're using the cauliflower right away, proceed with the recipe as described below. If you're storing it for another day, transfer it to a storage container and place it in the fridge. Ensure that you use the cauliflower over the next 4 to 5 days.

To prepare the dressing, in a small bowl, add the olive oil, white wine vinegar, lemon, basil, oregano and salt. Whisk until the ingredients are combined.

Cooking Method

Add the quinoa, cucumber, cherry tomatoes, scallions, celery and cauliflower to a serving bowl. Pour the dressing over the salad and toss.

Enjoy one serving of this salad as a side dish or two servings as a main dish. Unused servings can be transferred to a storage container and placed in the fridge overnight.

> ### Meal Prep Note
>
> If you wish to prepare this bowl for a few days, once you combine all the bowl ingredients but before adding the dressing, split the bowl into four separate servings. Place them in single-portion containers and store them in the fridge.

Grilled Halloumi Couscous Bowl

Yield: 2 servings

Halloumi cheese originates from Greece and nutritionally is considered a high protein cheese, typically made from sheep or goat milk or a combination of the two. The taste is intense and the texture is chewy, so it makes a great meat alternative.

Although you can eat halloumi straight from the package, this cheese is the best when grilled or panfried. The crispiness you get around the edges is just too good to miss!

Ingredients

1 cup (173 g) couscous

1 lemon, squeezed, with the juice divided

2 cups (480 ml) boiling water

1 tsp Himalayan salt

Avocado or olive oil spray

8 oz (226 g) halloumi cheese, sliced

1 cup (20 g) arugula

½ cup (90 g) olives, sliced

1 cup (150 g) cherry tomatoes, sliced in half

2 Persian cucumbers, sliced

1 tbsp (15 ml) olive oil

Prep Ahead

In a medium mixing bowl with a lid, add the couscous, juice from ½ lemon, water and salt. Stir the couscous, cover it and let it sit for at least 20 minutes or overnight. Remove the lid and fluff the couscous with a fork.

Cooking Method

In a nonstick grill pan, spray some avocado oil. When it's warm, add the sliced halloumi cheese. Grill it for about 3 minutes on one side, then flip it and grill it for another 2 minutes on the other side. Set it aside while you prepare the base of the bowl.

In a large mixing bowl, add the prepared couscous, arugula, olives, cherry tomatoes and cucumbers. Stir the salad, then add the juice from the other lemon half and the olive oil and toss it to combine.

Split the couscous into two single servings and add the grilled halloumi on top.

Enjoy one serving fresh and place the other one in a glass container with a lid and store it in the fridge for the next day.

Taco Bowl

with Roasted Veggies, Quinoa and Beans

Yield: 1 serving or 2 small servings

This bowl is a true nutrient powerhouse! From protein and fiber to good fats and antioxidants, this plant-based bowl will keep your tummy happy and nourished for a good part of the day. Sweet potatoes and broccoli both take about the same time to roast, which really saves time when it comes to preparing this dish. Since we are using olive oil on the roasted veggies as well as the mushrooms, you do not need to add any additional oil to this bowl at the end. Salsa and lime do it all!

Ingredients

1 medium sweet potato, cubed (about 1 cup [134 g])

1½ cups (136 g) broccoli florets

Olive oil spray

1 tsp cumin

1 tsp chili powder blend

1 tsp olive oil

1 cup (80 g) sliced shiitake mushrooms

Pinch of salt

1 whole grain or almond flour tortilla (optional)

½ cup (93 g) cooked quinoa (page 13)

½ cup (86 g) canned black beans, drained and rinsed

¼ avocado, sliced

⅓ cup (80 ml) salsa

½ large lime, squeezed

Cooking Method

Preheat the oven to 425°F (220°C). Line a sheet pan with parchment paper and add the sweet potato and broccoli. Spray the veggies with olive oil and toss them. Sprinkle cumin and chili powder on top and mix them again. Bake the veggies for about 20 to 25 minutes, or until the sweet potato softens.

In the meantime, add the olive oil to a nonstick or cast-iron pan and when it's warm, add the mushrooms. Add a pinch of salt and sauté the mushrooms for about 5 minutes.

If you're using a tortilla, toss it in the pan lightly until it's warm. Place it inside a bowl and then add the quinoa, beans, roasted sweet potato, broccoli, mushrooms, sliced avocado and salsa. Squeeze some lime on top and serve it fresh.

Meal Prep Notes

If you wish to make this as a meal prep for the next day, omit the avocado, as it will brown in the fridge overnight. Once you prepare everything as described above, allow it to cool down completely, then place it in a storage container. The next day, just add the avocado (and the tortilla, if you're using it) and enjoy it straight from the fridge.

Breakfast Buffet

How we start our day truly defines how we feel throughout the day. Some of us like to sit down and have a solid breakfast, some like to pick something up on the go and others love to bring breakfast to work. Whichever type you are, in this section you will find something that you will truly love. Each of these recipes is carefully crafted so that it is not only delicious but nutritious as well. Whether you choose to make one of the delicious Overnight Oats Three Ways (page 168), the Veggie Frittata with Feta (page 153) or a Boiled Egg Breakfast Bowl (page 159), any of these breakfast choices will keep you happy and full!

Veggie Frittata
with Feta

Yield: 2 servings

One of the best ways to add veggies to your breakfast is by making a breakfast frittata. This hearty and savory breakfast is really satisfying—and nutritious enough that it can be enjoyed multiple times a week. To make it more interesting, you can play around with different vegetables so you can feel like it is a new breakfast dish all over again. Some of my favorite combinations besides the one here are spinach, scallion and goat cheese; leeks, tomatoes and feta; and yellow onion and zucchini.

Ingredients

1 tbsp (15 ml) olive oil

1 small green or red pepper, finely chopped (about ¾ cup [112 g])

½ cup (35 g) oyster mushrooms, finely chopped

1 scallion, green and white part, finely chopped (about ¼ cup [12 g])

3 eggs, beaten

¼ cup (60 ml) coconut milk

½ tsp Himalayan salt

½ tsp dried basil

Black pepper to taste (optional)

¼ cup (38 g) feta cheese

Cooking Method

Add the olive oil to a nonstick pan and when it's warm, add the green pepper, mushrooms and scallion. Sauté the veggies until they're soft, about 2 minutes.

While the veggies are sautéing, add the eggs to a small mixing bowl and beat them until they're unified. Add the coconut milk along with the salt, basil and black pepper (if you're using it) and mix them until everything is well incorporated.

Pour the egg batter into the pan with the veggies and stir until the veggies are distributed evenly. Lower the heat to low and cover it with a lid. Cook the frittata for about 3 minutes or until the eggs look cooked through. Sprinkle the feta cheese on top, cover the frittata again and let it rest for 1 minute.

Meal Prep Notes

Enjoy half of the dish fresh for breakfast, and allow the rest of the frittata to cool down. Once it has cooled, place it in a container with a lid. Store it in the fridge. When you're ready to have it the next day, warm it up or have it cold straight out of the fridge.

Gluten-Free High Protein Pancakes

with Blueberry Chia Jam

Yield: 2 servings (10 mini pancakes)

I always like having some pancakes on hand, especially the protein- and fiber-loaded ones, because they make a great snack the next day. In fact, I'm not sure if you've ever had cold pancakes from the fridge, but if you add some fruit to them and pour fresh maple syrup on top, it tastes like the best dessert!

Perhaps you've never tried sweet potatoes in pancake batter and you may be wary, but don't worry; it just adds sweetness to the batter and you can't really taste the potato. Because of the oat flour—which has a nutty flavor—and the peanut butter, the pancakes are neutral in taste, so you can really play around with toppings. These pancakes go with any topping you can imagine, from fresh fruit and maple syrup to Greek yogurt and agave syrup to peanut butter and honey.

Ingredients

Blueberry Chia Jam

1¾ cups (260 g) frozen blueberries or any berries of your choice

2 tbsp (28 g) brown or coconut sugar

½ tsp vanilla extract

1⅓ cups (300 ml) water

2 tbsp (20 g) chia seeds

Pancakes

1 medium roasted sweet potato (about ½ cup [125 g] mashed)

2 eggs, beaten

¼ cup (60 ml) unsweetened almond milk or any plant-based milk

¼ cup (60 ml) creamy peanut butter

½ cup (60 g) oat flour

1 tsp baking powder

Coconut oil spray

Meal Prep Notes

Plate one serving of pancakes on a plate along with 2 tablespoons (30 ml) of the chia jam that you prepared the day before. Allow the second serving of pancakes to cool down, then place it in a storage container along with 2 table-spoons of chia jam.

The next day, the pancakes should be eaten cold, and because you added the jam on top the night before, it will taste like the best cake!

Prep Ahead

In a small saucepan, add the frozen blueberries, sugar and vanilla extract. Stir until everything is incorporated, then add the water in. Bring it to a boil, then cover it with a lid and lower the heat to medium-low. Cook the jam for about 15 minutes or until most of the liquid evaporates.

Add the chia seeds in, stir it well, then cover the jam with the lid and let it rest for about 10 minutes. Allow the jam to cool down and then transfer it to a glass jar with a lid. Store it in the fridge overnight, or up to 5 days.

While the chia jam is cooking, preheat the oven to 425°F (220°C).

Split the sweet potato in half by cutting it lengthwise. Line a small baking sheet with parchment paper and place the sweet potato with the cut sides down. Bake the sweet potato for about 20 minutes, or until you can pierce a fork through it. Take the potato out and let it cool down to room temperature. Peel the skin off the potato, then place it in a small glass jar until you're ready to use it the next day, or for up to 3 days.

Cooking Method

In a high-speed blender, add the eggs, unsweetened almond milk, sweet potato, peanut butter, oat flour and baking powder. Blend them until you get a smooth texture similar to that of American pancake batter. Heat up a nonstick pan, grease it with some coconut oil and then scoop out small pancakes from the batter with a tablespoon. Cook the pancakes like you usually would.

Corn Muffins
with Prosciutto and Feta

Yield: 6 muffins (3 servings)

Growing up in Serbia, one of my favorite things to eat was proja, or corn bread. In contrast to corn bread in the USA, proja is savory rather than sweet, and it's typically eaten for breakfast or dinner with some yogurt or a salad. During the holidays, corn bread is made with cheese and served instead of bread.

The recipe below is made with prosciutto and feta, but instead of feta, you can use farmer's cheese and instead of prosciutto, you can use ham or smoked turkey (½ cup [145 g]) as well as chopped spinach (about 1 cup [30 g]). At times I add both prosciutto and spinach, and in case you would like to try that, just add additional liquid such as yogurt or plant-based milk (5.5 oz [160 ml]).

These tasty and nutritious corn muffins are high in protein and fiber and make a great prepared meal for bring-to-work breakfast and snack options. One great thing about these muffins is that they are delicious even when cold out of the fridge.

Ingredients

Olive oil or avocado oil spray

2 eggs, beaten

5.5 oz (155 g) Greek yogurt

¼ cup (60 ml) olive oil

½ cup (75 g) feta cheese, crumbled

1 cup (160 g) polenta

¼ cup (31 g) spelt flour, or any flour of your choice

1 tsp baking powder

2.6 oz (75 g, about 4 slices) prosciutto, chopped

Cooking Method

Preheat the oven to 400°F (200°C). Spray a muffin pan with olive oil and set it aside.

In a small mixing bowl, add the eggs, Greek yogurt, olive oil and feta. Beat the mixture until everything is well combined. Add the polenta, spelt flour and baking powder and stir until combined. Add the prosciutto in, then stir the batter and pour it into the muffin pan.

Bake the muffins for about 16 minutes, or until a toothpick comes out clean. Once you take the muffins out of the oven, let them cool for about 10 minutes.

Meal Prep Notes

To save any leftover servings, allow the muffins to cool down completely, then place them in a storage container with a lid or in a silicone bag and refrigerate them. Enjoy the muffins cold or warm. These muffins also freeze well for up to 1 month. To defrost them, let the muffins sit out overnight at room temperature. You may reheat them in the microwave if you wish.

The batter for the muffins can be prepared ahead as well. Simply follow the directions above to mix the batter, then place it in a storage container with a lid. Refrigerate it overnight. When you're ready to make the muffins, transfer the batter to a muffin pan and bake them per the instructions above. The mixture may thicken in the fridge, and if that happens, add about ¼ cup (60 ml) of water or liquid yogurt to the batter before baking it.

Boiled Egg Breakfast Bowl

Yield: 2 servings

Eggs are a wonderful source of protein and unsaturated fats, which are good for our health, especially our heart. Eggs also contain vitamins B6 and B12 as well as vitamins A and D. All this makes them a great breakfast choice, as they not only provide us with an energy boost, but they keep us full longer due to their high protein and fat content. I love keeping boiled eggs in the fridge during the week and using them for breakfast, adding them to salads for lunch or enjoying them with some freshly cut peppers and cucumbers as a snack.

Ingredients

4 eggs

2 cups (40 g) arugula

½ cup (55 g) carrots, shredded

½ English cucumber, sliced thin

8 black olives, pitted

2 tbsp (30 ml) olive oil

2 tsp lemon juice

1 tsp black sesame seeds

Himalayan salt (optional)

Cooking Method

Fill up a small saucepan halfway with water and bring it to a boil. Slowly add the eggs one by one, using a spoon. Cook them for about 8 to 10 minutes, depending how you like the eggs cooked. For soft-boiled eggs, cook them for 8 minutes, and for very well-cooked eggs, cook them for 10 minutes.

Remove the pan from the heat, pour out the hot water and pour in cold water right away. This process of running the cooked eggs under cold water helps the eggs peel easier. Peel the eggs and set them aside.

In a serving bowl, add 1 cup (20 g) of arugula, ¼ cup (28 g) of shredded carrots, ¼ English cucumber and 4 olives. Drizzle 1 tablespoon (15 ml) of olive oil along with 1 teaspoon of lemon juice. Add 2 peeled eggs to a bowl, then add some sesame seeds and salt if you're using it. Enjoy this one serving of breakfast right away and save the second for tomorrow morning.

Meal Prep Notes

Once the eggs cool down, peel them and place them in a small glass container with a lid. In another glass container, add the arugula, carrots, olives and English cucumber. Store it in the fridge. The next day, when you are ready to serve it, drizzle 1 tablespoon (15 ml) of olive oil and 1 teaspoon of lemon juice on top of the arugula and carrots, add the eggs on top and enjoy!

Baked Polenta
with Spinach and Tofu

Yield: 6–8 servings

Polenta is a staple breakfast offering in Serbia but in other European countries and in the USA is prepared as a side dish or as part of the main meal. In fact, when I moved to the States, I was surprised to find polenta topped with truffled mushrooms or sautéed spinach being served with steak or roasted chicken. All I knew before was that polenta was served with yogurt for breakfast.

I added tofu to this recipe because I wanted to up the protein game in this breakfast option. I also used vegan feta cheese, which is typically made with coconut oil or cream, to add some good fats to the dish as well. Dark leafy greens, spinach leaves, are added for the antioxidants, and finally eggs add another wonderful source of protein.

This baked polenta is also a great party appetizer instead of serving bread. It goes wonderfully with ham or prosciutto and fresh tomatoes. It also makes a great add-on to any BBQ—perhaps you might try it with the chicken from the Grilled Chicken Gyros with Homemade Gyro Spice (page 72), Not Your Traditional Greek Salad (page 61) or Turkey Chili (page 107).

Ingredients

3 eggs, beaten

½ cup (120 ml) almond milk

⅛ cup (30 ml) grapeseed or olive oil

1 cup (160 g) polenta

½ (14-oz [400-g]) package silken or regular tofu, crumbled

⅔ cup (100 g) vegan feta, crumbled

1 cup (30 g) spinach, chopped

1 tbsp (9 g) sesame seeds

Cooking Method

Preheat the oven to 400°F (200°C). You can use either a 9 x 9–inch (23 x 23–cm) pan with parchment paper for baking or a cast-iron pan.

Add the eggs, almond milk and oil to a mixing bowl. Stir until they are well combined and then add the polenta, tofu and vegan feta. Stir in the spinach. Pour the mixture into the pan, sprinkle the sesame seeds on top and bake it for about 20 to 25 minutes, or until a toothpick comes out clean.

> **Meal Prep Notes**
>
> Allow the polenta to cool for about 5 minutes, then cut it into six or eight slices. Place one serving on a plate with some vegan Greek yogurt or cashew yogurt on top. Enjoy it warm.
>
> Allow the rest to cool down completely, then place the cut slices into a storage container with a lid. Place it in the fridge and store it over the next 3 days. Polenta can be eaten cold the next day, or you can warm it up for a few seconds in the microwave.

Maple Quinoa Porridge
with Cashew Milk

Yield: 2 servings

When we hear quinoa, we think hearty and savory. But because this high protein, high fiber pseudograin is very neutral in taste, once you add something sweet to it, it magically transforms! I suggest you try adding some cashew milk or unsweetened almond milk, a touch of coconut sugar, maple syrup or honey, and fresh fruit, such as berries. And the best part about this porridge is that you can have it during all seasons by simply swapping in fruits that are currently in season.

Ingredients

Porridge

1½ cups (360 ml) cashew milk

2 cups (370 g) cooked quinoa (page 13)

1 tsp vanilla extract

2 tbsp (30 ml) maple syrup or coconut sugar

Seasonal Toppings

Fresh berries and unsweetened coconut flakes (summer/spring)

Caramelized bananas or baked apples, walnuts and cinnamon (fall/winter)

Cooking Method

Add the cashew milk to a small pot and bring it to a boil. Add the quinoa, vanilla extract and maple syrup or coconut sugar and stir. Boil it for just a couple of minutes, or until the quinoa is warm enough to your taste.

Add one serving of porridge to a small bowl and top with ¼ cup (37 g) of fresh berries and 1 tablespoon (4 g) of unsweetened coconut flakes.

Meal Prep Notes

Enjoy half of the dish fresh for breakfast, and allow the rest of the porridge to cool down. Once cooled, place it (without toppings) into a container or jar. Store it in the fridge.

When you're ready to have it the next day, warm it up on the stove and add the toppings. Quinoa may soak up all the liquid as it's stored, so to make it thinner in texture again like it was when you made it, add a few tablespoons of any plant-based milk. You can also eat this cold as you would with chia pudding. It's really delicious that way as well.

Gluten-Free Blueberry Lemon Breakfast Cake

Yield: 9 small pieces

This recipe is perfect for the mornings when you crave something sweet. Or perhaps you love having a nice cookie or a pastry with your coffee in the afternoon but don't want to drag yourself down with butter- and sugar-filled white flour alternatives. The combination of oat and almond flour gives this cake a really nice nutty flavor, but at the same time it is nicely offset with blueberries and lemon. Maple syrup ties it all in for a perfect and decadent bite.

Ingredients

1 cup (120 g) oat flour

1½ cups (180 g) almond flour

½ tsp baking powder

½ tsp baking soda

2 eggs

⅓ cup (80 ml) unsweetened almond milk

½ cup (120 ml) maple syrup

⅓ cup (80 ml) melted coconut oil

1 tsp vanilla extract

1 lemon, squeezed

¾ cup (111 g) fresh blueberries

Cooking Method

Preheat the oven to 400°F (200°C). Line a 9 x 9–inch (23 x 23–cm) baking tray with parchment paper. Alternatively, you can use a small bread loaf pan.

In a mixing bowl, add the oat flour, almond flour, baking powder and baking soda. In a separate bowl, add all the wet ingredients: eggs, almond milk, maple syrup, coconut oil, vanilla extract and lemon juice. Mix them well, then add the batter to the dry mixture. Sprinkle some flour on the blueberries to help keep the blueberries intact while baking, then stir them in. Bake the cake for 25 minutes, or until a toothpick comes out clean.

Meal Prep Notes

Allow the cake to cool down to room temperature, cut it into small squares and then place them in a glass container with a lid. Store the cake in the fridge over the next 3 to 5 days. This cake is meant to be enjoyed cold. As it stays in the fridge, the flavors marinate even more.

Gluten-Free Homemade Bread

with Buckwheat, Oat and Sesame

Yield: 10 slices

The rich, nutty flavor of buckwheat and the sweetness of oats are perfectly combined with sesame, which brings out both the nuttiness and sweetness in this bread. Yet a very neutral taste is the end result! Soy yogurt is used in combination with baking soda and baking powder instead of yeast, making this bread even more nutritious.

The bread is very soft and moist on the inside, but the crust is a bit firmer so it stays intact. It's great for sandwiches, for a delicious avocado toast, for peanut butter and banana toast or for PB&J (with my delicious Blueberry Chia Jam [page 154]). You can also serve it with a Veggie Frittata with Feta (page 153) or Boiled Egg Breakfast Bowl (page 159). And if you love toasted bread with your soup or stew, try this bread with my delicious High Protein Fagioli Soup with Chickpea Pasta (page 39) or Italian Wedding Soup with Turkey and Quinoa (page 33).

Fun fact: Despite its name, buckwheat is not related to wheat and is gluten free, making it an excellent alternative for those with gluten sensitivities or following a gluten-free diet.

Ingredients

1 cup (120 g) oat flour
1 cup (120 g) buckwheat
½ cup (64 g) cornstarch
¾ cup (108 g) sesame seeds
2 tsp Himalayan salt
1 tsp baking soda
1 tsp baking powder
2½ cups (600 ml) soy yogurt

Prep Ahead

In a mixing bowl, add the oat flour, buckwheat and cornstarch along with the sesame seeds, Himalayan salt, baking soda and baking powder. Stir to combine them, then add the soy yogurt. Mix them until you get a unified dough. The dough will be sticky and runny, but do not worry. Cover the bowl with plastic and place it in the fridge overnight.

Cooking Method

Preheat the oven to 400°F (200°C). Line a 9 x 9–inch (23 x 23–cm) pan or a bread pan with parchment paper.

Take the dough out of the fridge, stir it once and transfer it to the pan. Make sure the dough is evenly spread across the bread pan. Bake the bread for 35 to 40 minutes. (To ensure the bread is baked, test it with a toothpick to see if it comes out clean.) Take the bread out of the oven and the baking pan and let it rest on a cooling rack for at least 20 minutes before cutting it.

Meal Prep Notes

The bread can be stored at room temperature for a day wrapped in a dish towel or a piece of parchment paper. The next day, wrap the bread in parchment paper and place it in the fridge, where it can stay fresh for up to 5 days. You can also cut the bread into slices and freeze it in Ziploc® bags. To thaw it, just take the bread out and keep it at room temperature. Another option is to toast it straight from the freezer.

Overnight Oats
Three Ways

Yield: 2 servings

Oats in a jar are such a lifesaver when it comes to preparing your breakfast or a snack ahead of time and having it ready to go when needed. Simply add oats with your favorite toppings in a jar with a lid, close it and refrigerate it overnight. The next morning, grab a spoon, stir and your breakfast is ready! Oats prepared like this can stay fresh in the fridge for up to 4 days.

Below, I've shared three of my favorite flavor options for you to choose from. However, there are endless ways to use what you have on hand for unique toppings. Here is an easy formula you can follow to ensure that your breakfast is properly balanced:

Oats

1 additional protein/good fat source (chia, flax, hemp, whey or plant-based protein, nuts and seeds or nut butter)

1 serving of fruit of your choice

Liquid (water, plant-based milk, Greek yogurt)

Ingredients

Coconut Chia Oats

1 cup (90 g) rolled oats
1 tbsp (8 g) coconut protein
½ tbsp (7 g) coconut sugar
1 cup (240 ml) coconut milk

Blueberry Chia Oats

1 cup (90 g) rolled oats
1 tbsp (10 g) chia seeds
½ cup (74 g) frozen blueberries or any type of berries
1 tbsp (15 ml) honey
¼ tsp vanilla extract
1¼ cups (300 ml) water

Flax Seed Maple Oats

1 cup (90 g) rolled oats
1 tbsp (10 g) whole flax seeds
1–2 tbsp (15–30 ml) maple syrup
⅔ cup (160 ml) Greek yogurt
⅔ cup (160 ml) water

Cooking Method

In a small mixing bowl, add the oats and all the dry ingredients, then add in the liquid. Stir it well to combine and split the oatmeal mixture into two jars. Cover the jars with lids and refrigerate them overnight.

The next day, just add your favorite toppings and enjoy!

Meal Prep Notes

In case you wish to prepare and enjoy the oats on the same day, the soaking process for the oats takes about 30 minutes. Alternatively, you can warm up the liquid you are using and enjoy your oats within a few minutes.

Wholesome Smoothie Blends

Yield: 1 serving

Smoothies are not only great as a healthy refreshment in the summer months, but they also make a great breakfast on the go. And there is nothing easier than preparing your smoothies ahead of time. Simply place all the veggies and fruits you wish to use for your smoothie into individual Ziploc® or silicone bags and freeze them overnight. To make the smoothie, just add the contents of one bag to a blender with the rest of the fresh ingredients (e.g., plant-based milk, coconut water or yogurt) and blend.

Ingredients

Peanut Butter Banana

1 banana

1 cup (30 g) baby spinach

1 Persian cucumber, cut in half

1 tbsp (16 g) peanut butter, or any nut butter

1 cup (240 ml) vanilla almond milk

Blueberry Kale

1 cup (67 g) kale

1 banana

⅓ cup (49 g) blueberries

1 cup (240 ml) unsweetened almond milk

1½ tbsp (22 ml) maple syrup

Peachy Avocado

½ peach

⅓ avocado

¾ cup (108 g) whole strawberries or raspberries

1 cup (240 ml) coconut water

1 tbsp (15 ml) honey

Cooking Method

Add all the wholesome smoothie ingredients to a high-speed blender and blend until they are smooth. Enjoy your smoothie right away while it's fresh. If you wish to save some of the smoothie for later on, place it in a jar and refrigerate it.

Acknowledgments

The opportunity to write another cookbook was something I could only dream of. This cookbook is not just a collection of my most delicious recipes but also a true labor of love. There were countless hours spent experimenting with flavors, techniques and ingredients. In between the delicious lunches and dinners that came out of this cookbook, there were some failed recipes too. And this is where my love for healthy food and strong desire to inspire others came through.

This book truly would not have been possible without the support, inspiration and assistance of many incredible people in my life.

To my husband, Boris, who has been my biggest support for over 20 years now. Thank you for always believing in me and for supporting all of my crazy ideas like leaving my auditing career to become a nutrition and health coach. Thank you for trusting me and always being there. And above all, thank you for giving me our beautiful children. I'm grateful for the life we have built together.

And to my kids, Mia and Luka, I know I was not always the most popular mom with your "green" school lunches, but I promise you, it was all for you and your future. Your health and happiness have always been and will always be my priority.

To my parents. To my dad, who raised me to be the strong woman I am today. And to my mom, whose words of support always follow me and protect me.

To my little brother. The older we are, the more I appreciate you and your love for me and my kids. And to my Lari, thank you for testing some of the recipes for "tetka." Without you, these recipes would not be the same. Love you always.

To my friends. You know who you are and what you mean to me. The older I am, the more I appreciate all of you and the time we spend together.

To my editors at Page Street Publishing. Thank you for giving me the opportunity to pour all of my love for healthy food and cooking into another cookbook. Your guidance and support helped enormously for this cookbook to see the light of day.

And to all of you beautiful people reading this. Thank you for trusting me to guide you toward your own healthier lives. Cheers to all of you!

About the Author

As a certified nutrition and health coach, Snezana Paucinac has been fortunate enough to work with many incredible clients and lead them toward becoming the very best and healthiest versions of themselves. Her love for healthy living and nutrition led Snezana to create a very successful social media platform, where she shares her nutritious and delicious recipes, meal preparing ideas and healthy living tips.

Her popular recipes resulted in her publishing her first book, *5-Ingredient Clean Eating Cookbook*, which gained a lot of popularity right from the start. This cookbook was a compilation of simple, clean dishes that were easy to make yet very wholesome and tasty. In Snezana's work with nutrition clients, she realized that there was a need for more guidance when it came to meal planning and being organized in the kitchen, and that is exactly how the concept for this meal prep cookbook was born.

With her blog and this cookbook, Snezana hopes to inspire people to live healthy lives, see the beauty and joy in home-cooked meals and take care of themselves. Because at the end of the day, being healthy is not a diet or a chore but a beautiful lifestyle.

After living in the USA for over 20 years, Snezana moved back to her hometown of Belgrade, Serbia, where she currently resides with her husband Boris, her two kids Mia and Luka and their bulldog Toby. Being a mom and a wife, traveling and building a beautiful life with her family are things Snezana cherishes every day.

Index